Lanterns That Lit Our World

Lanterns That Lit Our World

How to Identify, Date, and Restore Old Railroad, Marine, Fire, Carriage, Farm, and Other Lanterns

ANTHONY HOBSON

Ninth Printing, October, 1996

Text Copyright © 1991 by Anthony Hobson

Library of Congress Catalog Card Number: 89-81427
    ISBN: 0-9614876-5-8

Published in the United States of America by
    Golden Hill Press, Inc., Spencertown, New York 12165
This book was set in Goudy Old Style
    by Kath Moran of North Wing Studios, Hudson, New York

To my wife, Cathy, for her help during the many, many hours spent doing research and visiting antique dealers, antique shows, and flea markets. But most of all for her love, patience, and understanding.

Table of Contents

Preface

This book provides the kind of information that would have been helpful to me when I first began collecting lanterns. It will give you some idea of the rarity of a particular lantern you may be curious about. In most cases, it will show you how the lantern originally looked, so that you will know if a part is missing before you buy. It will help you evaluate the lantern's condition and restore it to close to its original appearance. You will get some idea of a lantern's age and what it was probably used for or, at least, intended to be used for. (For example, not all railroad-style lanterns were used by the railroad.) You will get a general sense of what price category it falls into. The book will show you how lanterns work and can be put into working order.

Information of this sort is invaluable to the lantern collector or admirer, but much of it is not generally available. I know from experience the frustration of trying to find it out. As a collector, I have spent years going to auctions, flea markets, museums, railroad shows, and antique shops and from this learned much about which of the old lanterns are still available. From repairing and restoring them, I have also learned a good deal. But these sources have their limitations. For instance, it became obvious to me that there were several basic lantern designs and within each of these categories, many different lantern styles. But when and why the various designs and changes came about was a mystery. The available books on "lanterns" covered mostly the indoor, interior lamps, with their attractive colored-or etched- glass globes and bases. My interest was in the outdoor, portable lantern or lamp, used both in and out of doors, but functional in all kinds of weather. While brief write-ups in various encyclopedias covered one or another aspect of lantern lighting, design, or manufacture, these touched on only small pieces of the puzzle, and even some of this material I have now found to be contradicted by what I learned from primary sources during my own research.

I next turned to those few 19th-and 20th-century lantern manufacturers that are still in business today, sometimes under a name different from the one that appeared on their old lanterns. With several of these — most notably, Dietz and, to a lesser extent, Adlake — I at last found a great fund of information, not only about these companies but also about earlier ones they had absorbed or done business with. These led me to still other manufacturer's names and to further places to research.

For over a year and a half, I collected or copied and then systematically went through old records: interdepartmental memos; materials lists; illustrated catalogs; sales brochures; bills of lading; invoices; correspondence; patent drawings and files; shipping records; and, finally, diaries kept by R. E. Dietz. All were helpful. Sifting back and forth, from one to another, I was able to reconstruct a reasonably accurate picture of a century and more of lantern manufacture, sales, and use. I say "reasonably" because some of the material was so fragile that it was hard to read and impossible, unfortunately, to reproduce here. The final result includes specifications, production dates, and uses of hundreds of lanterns produced in the 19th and 20th centuries.

I also learned much about the makers of these lanterns and about the remarkable role lanterns played in American commerce, industry, and domestic culture. It is my hope that passing this information on to you, the reader, will help kindle an interest in saving, collecting, restoring, and cherishing this once indispensable American artifact. It is my hope also, in writing about these old lanterns, to learn more from reader feedback, for this book cannot, of course, be the "final word" on American lanterns. Too many of them have perished without having been documented and too many relevant records and bits of information have been lost through neglect, disinterest and the passage of time. By now, in this late 20th century, new bits of information about old lanterns are as likely to turn up by chance as through attempts at systematic research. For this reason I welcome any information you, the reader, can share with me about a specific lantern, or its use or manufacturer or manufacturing method. Perhaps from a lantern in your garage or basement, or in a childhood memory, you hold the key to some obscure bit of lantern history! Meantime, I offer this book to help those of you who already collect lanterns or are interested in doing so, by providing you with this information in a form that will make it easier for you to evaluate the lanterns you find or own.

Acknowledgments

A very special thank you to Penny Macrides, Administrative Secretary, R. E. Dietz Company, without whose help this book could not have been written.

Thank you to the following people for their help with historic and manufacturing information:

To Edward Reynolds, President, R. E. Dietz Company, for granting me permission to read and photostat all and any records I needed from the Dietz archives; Hugh Dietz, Vice-President, R. E. Dietz Company; and Thomas Vause, National Sales Manager, R. E. Dietz Company.

To Leroy Ott, President, and Paul Gingerich, Sales Manager, Adams and Westlake, Ltd. And to Leo F. Bolden, Vice-President of Operations Wheeling Stamping Company, all of whom gave me material that helped my research.

To David Gluck, Administrator, Fireman's Home, Hudson, New York, and Robert Dalzell, Curator of the American Museum of Fire Fighting, Hudson, New York, who gave me access to exhibits and information.

To Donald Goldberg, who did research in the Newberry Library, Chicago, Illinois, to answer my questions on Chicago companies. To Cynthia Millar, of the St. Louis, Missouri, public library staff, who gave me information on a St. Louis company.

To the many antiques shop owners in New York, Connecticut, and Massachusetts who allowed me to photograph their lanterns.

To Jerry Fox, a Vermont collector of lanterns, who shared his knowledge about them with me, and to Charles Klimek, a New York railroad engineer, who gave me additonal information on railroad signals.

To all the people along the way who contributed information recalled from their childhood memories, and to everyone else who helped in ways too numerous to mention.

Finally, to Mary Zander, my editor, grateful appreciation. Her expertise and relentless pursuit of perfection turned my shambles of a manuscript into this book.

Introduction:
A Brief History of American Lanterns

To truly appreciate lanterns, one must remember that not so long ago there were no electric lights. Being able to see at night, except by brightest moonlight, was a chancy business. America's early lights — the rush lights, Betty lamps, candles, and, later, oil lamps — all gave only minimal amounts of light indoors. And even the best interior oil lamps, with their tall, graceful glass chimneys, were not windproof or rainproof or truly portable, because the flame was too easily extinguished. Indeed, it is difficult to understand how our forebears accomplished as much as they did under such lighting conditions. It was only with the many developments in portable-lantern design and manufacture that we acquired the consistent, highly mobile, and weatherproof lighting that we needed in order to see and work and travel in our world during nighttime. Later, lanterns were in turn supplanted — by gas lighting, by electricity, by battery-powered flashlights. But during the height of America's expansion and the blossoming of its technology, commerce, and industry, lamps and lanterns were, for a while, the quintessential lighting devices.

The word "lantern" originally referred specifically to the translucent or transparent case or covering, such as horn, that protected the candle or other flame from wind and rain. The term "lamp" referred to the actual light source. The words now are often used interchangeably, but "lantern" came to mean, more specifically, a well-protected, usually portable light source used out of doors under all kinds of conditions. This book is about such outdoor lanterns.

How Lanterns Were Used

Lanterns made it possible for Americans to do more things round the clock and in all seasons. As we developed new forms of transportation, we needed to be able to move, unhampered by the limitations of earlier lamps, by means of carriage, canal and steamboat, railroad and automobile. The faster we were able to go, the more we needed better lighting. Lanterns helped us keep to our new pace and utilize our new technologies. In turn, the discovery of new fuels, manufacturing techniques, and uses for lanterns brought changes in how they looked and functioned, as they were redesigned to adapt to new circumstances. More than many other 19th- and early-20th-century artifacts, lanterns reflect, in their myriad forms, the changes in American culture and commerce. These were years of constant inventiveness, and lanterns were in the thick of it.

We hear these times evoked in the language of the old sales catalogs. Here, lantern names and uses, detailed in the now quaint Victorian style of the advertisements, mirror our every domestic, commercial, industrial, and recreational activity. They speak of babies' night lanterns and of blizzards, of livery stables and summer resorts. Of sailors doing their work at night on the dark sea. Of locomotives, with lanterns for headlights racing, by yester- day's standards of speed, through the night across the new continent. The mills and factories of our industrial revolution could be operated late into the night. The carriage lanterns on the dashboards of buggies and wagons lit the way of country doctors on stormy rural roads. Buoys stayed depend- ably lit on our waterways, and railroad bridges, opened in the dark, sig- naled danger with their red lanterns. The Coast Guard and lighthouse keepers used lanterns in their long-burning searchlights. Policemen could use their lanterns to flash for help, and lanterns lit our streets in many towns. The social gatherings outside our homes — cornhuskings and barn dances, hayrides and camp meetings — were illuminated by lantern light.

Lantern Design and Development

Lanterns were not only useful but often attractive as well. Commen- tators on 19th-century American culture have noted the beauty of many of our commercial and industrial designs. Large or small objects — ships and locomotives, machines and tools, domestic artifacts — frequently displayed a grace unnecessary to their basic function. Lanterns certainly belong among such artifacts. Because of their materials, lines, and structures, many are very handsome. Of course, attractiveness varies with the type of lantern. The more monolithic railroad lanterns, for example, are rather uninteresting in their forms and finishes. But a brass conductor's lantern or a marine lantern or a carriage lamp, polished and with globe intact, can be

Paul Revere Lantern.   Fire Company.
Before 1830.   1815 – 1840.   Domestic. 1815 – 1840.

a breathtaking sight, and the many embellishments on basic lantern design resulted in a great variety of forms and styles. This range of shapes and materials offers the admirer or collector of lanterns much to explore and to appreciate.

In the century and a half of lantern use, a number of major developments altered or improved lantern lighting. In the early 1800's, lanterns were still wooden or metal boxes with glass, horn, or metal sides, with a candle as the usual light source. By the 1820s, whale oil became more widely available. Lamps with a wick and a font and burning this oil gave a better light than did the lanterns then in use, and they began to replace them. By the 1830s, as the quality of glass improved, lamps with glass globes and metal bases and tops became common. By 1850, wire guards were being used to protect glass globes, making the lantern more sturdy and thus more popular and suitable for outdoor work.

Before lanterns began to be mass produced, in the mid-19th century, they were manufactured on a somewhat random basis, by local blacksmiths, tinsmiths or coppersmiths, or by small hardware manufacturing companies as part of a line of products. Often individually designed and made, the same model could vary from lantern to lantern. Some were even one of a kind. There usually were no markings on their bases or tops to identify their origins. These lanterns burned candles or whale oil. In the late 1850s, kerosene became widely available. Because of its cheapness and efficiency, and because of the rising cost of camphine during the Civil War, kerosene quickly emerged as the preeminent fuel. Lantern design began to be significantly modified to better use this fuel, and mass production of lanterns began.

Even then there was, not surprisingly, an overlap between old and new styles. The lanterns on this page and the previous page illustrate examples in the evolution of American lanterns, from the 18th-century tin lantern burning candles to the mid-19th-century dead-flame lantern with its glass globe and wire guard. After mid-century, lantern production soared and within a decade the number of designs and models had increased dramatically. In the late 1860s, the hot-blast design and, in the 1880s, the cold-blast design were developed; both styles persisted into the 20th century.

Wire Guards. 1840 – 1870.

Domestic, glass sides. Before 1850.

20th Century Lanterns

The period from the 1860s to about 1910 had been marked by improvements not only in design but also in manufacturing techniques and in quality. In the latter part of this period, improvements were very specialized. Inspired more by marketing considerations than by a need to improve lantern function, they were meant to attract specific buyers, such as the railroads or the Coast Guard. Lanterns by then were reliable and strong, there were fewer models, and their appearance was fairly standarized.

In essence, the lantern was now perfected. The only other significant change was in manufacturing techniques. In the late 1930s, lanterns began to appear "streamlined." That is, their parts were completely stamped out by machine, so there was no longer any need to hand solder individual parts together.

Lanterns continued to be used into the middle of the 20th century. Railroads, steamship lines, and general and highway contractors were major consumers. Among the general public the use of lanterns died out earlier. It persisted longer in rural areas, and even today those of us who live in the country may have a lantern or two tucked away in the basement, in case of a power outage.

The more fragile lanterns, those aimed at house, farm, barn, or general use, and the very oldest lanterns, have become scarce, as so many have perished. Also scarce are those that were part of a small or short-term production run. Nevertheless, there still are many lanterns waiting to be discovered and admired. Unfortunately, their origins and uses tend to be obscure or misunderstood. Yet, each has a story to tell. The purpose of this book is to help tell these stories and thus add to a fuller understanding of the important role lanterns have played in American life or, indeed, in life around the world.

Section I:
The Anatomy of Lanterns

How Lanterns Work: The Three Major Lantern Designs

Early to mid-19th-century lanterns were usually of the "dead-flame" type, although this name did not originate until mid-century or later, when it was used to contrast this lantern with the new hot-blast model. (Unlike the latter, the dead-flame lantern had no channeled, forced hot-air draft.)

John Irwin had patented the design for the hot-blast lantern in the mid-1860s. It was a major change in lantern design and had tremendous impact. By the 1880s Dietz had developed a cold-blast lantern. This was a progression from the hot-blast design, and channeled cold (fresh) air to the flame. Each of these was an improvement on the previous model, although the earlier ones were still manufactured and used in some areas. For example, the railroads continued to favor dead-flame lanterns long after hot-blast and cold-blast models had become widely available.

The impetus for many of these lantern design changes was the quest for the brightest possible light housed in the most windproof and rainproof lantern. Over the decades, large or small modifications in the wick, burner, air chamber, globe and globe plate, side tubes, bell, and lenses were intended to enhance the brilliance and strength of the flame.

To appreciate the effect of such design modifications, it helps to understand how the flame was produced in lanterns. The capillary action of the wick drew liquid fuel oil out of the lantern font. As it came up through the wick and met with the oxygen inside the globe, the fuel oil was vaporized over the exposed area of the wick. This vaporizing fuel was explosive. It began to burn when ignited and stayed lit as long as fuel remained.

One could regulate the amount of vaporized fuel available within the atmosphere of the globe by raising or lowering the wick, thereby also adjusting the height of the flame. If the lantern flame got too high, it went out, because it had cut off its own air (oxygen) supply by burning more oxygen than was available within the globe. A lesser oxygen shortage could suddenly reduce the flame size, but as soon as more oxygen was available, the flame leaped high again. This variation in oxygen-fuel mix caused the flickering of the flame, and in turn, the soot on the globe inner walls. In a well-designed lantern, the correct amount of air flowed though the globe continuously, giving, with the correct wick adjustment, an even air-fuel-mixed flame, which gave the most light and consumed fuel efficiently.

Dead-flame Lantern

This type of lantern was designed to eliminate, or minimize, the effect of drafts on the flame. A series of baffles inside the top (bell) above the top of the globe was positioned so that no top draft or wind could blow directly on the flame. Furthermore, bottom-draft holes were sized and located so that wind blown against the base was deflected by the font and

Dead-Flame Lantern

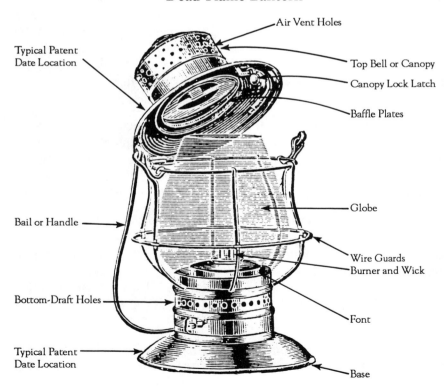

the globe base. This moderately controlled air flow resulted in a uniform, relatively nonflickering flame.

Hot-Blast Lantern

This type of lantern reused heated, partially burned air by mixing it with fresh air. Fresh air entered at the globe base through the perforated globe plate. As this air became heated and rose to the canopy above the globe, part of it, partially burned, flowed up through the canopy tube channel and was drawn, via down draft, through the side tubes and thence back up through the mesh inside the burner (see p. 20), where it mixed with more fresh air coming in. Because the partially burned air held carbon and

Hot-Blast Lantern

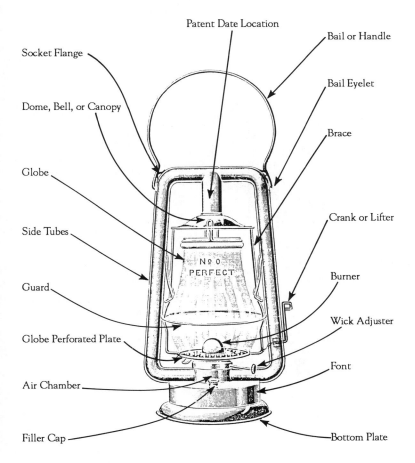

Patent Date Location

Bail or Handle

Socket Flange

Bail Eyelet

Dome, Bell, or Canopy

Brace

Globe

Side Tubes

Crank or Lifter

Guard

Burner

Globe Perforated Plate

Wick Adjuster

Air Chamber

Font

Filler Cap

Bottom Plate

No 0
PERFECT

other impurities, the flame of a hot-blast lantern tended to be yellow, not white. This flame was more controlled and therefore brighter, with better light output, than that of the dead-flame lantern. The concept of this design was a major step forward. All other design changes that followed were improvements on it.

Cold-Blast Lantern

This type of lantern fed only fresh air to the flame at the wick. All hot, burned air was expelled completely from the lantern, not recirculated as in a hot-blast lantern. The channeling of only fresh, oxygen-rich air to the flame yielded a white, more brilliant light. The candlepower of a cold-blast lantern was double that of a hot-blast lantern of the same wick size.

This illustration from a Dietz catalog is embellished with sales talk, but gives a very clear picture of the cold-blast functions.

Cold-Blast Lantern

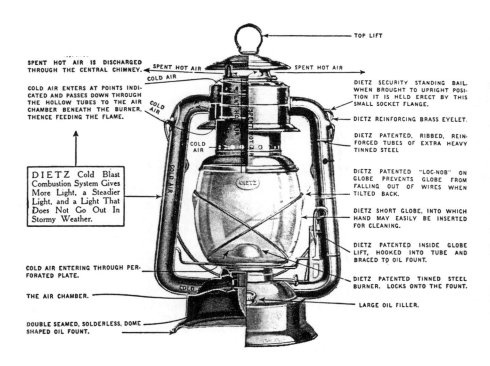

Lantern Parts: From Bottom to Top

This section illustrates and explains the different parts of the lantern that work together to produce, protect, and reflect the flame. Familiarity with how lanterns work will help you in identifying, buying, and restoring them. Both in your use of this book and in your lantern "explorations" at flea markets, antique stores, railroad shows, and museums, knowing the various parts of lanterns will help you spot those interesting details which may signal the rarer, more unusual lanterns, or those in better or more complete condition. These factors can affect a lantern's value.

Early lanterns did not have all the embellishments of later lanterns. Over the years each lantern part — the base, font, burner, wick, air holes, side tubes, globes, guards, dome, handles, and so on — was designed and redesigned. Besides making the lantern more efficient, these refinements were designed to give each new lantern the broadest possible market (e.g., burning several kinds of fuels), or to make it conform to the special needs of a particular market, such as railroads or contractors, or to render it more competitive in general by making it more attractive, or of obviously higher quality, or by giving it some new, probably proudly patented clip or lock or bail or "ventilating system" — some new feature that would supposedly give the manufacturer a sales edge and the buyer a better lantern.

In the pages that follow, the functions of each lantern part, in its simplest form, are indicated. Significant, widely adopted changes in design also are noted. Because there were so many variations in burners, these are given broader coverage.

Fonts

The main function of a lantern font was to hold the fuel. The font usually formed the base of the lamp, sometimes with a base plate under or around it. The shapes of these fonts added strength as well as beauty to the lanterns.

Fonts for dead-flame lanterns were often removable from the lantern base. If need be, they could be taken out from below — but sometimes from above — to be filled. Also, they could be replaced if they broke or became too corroded.

In hot-blast and cold-blast lanterns, the font typically was dome shaped and more likely to be an integral part of the lantern, rather than removable. Lanterns with dome-shaped fonts were stronger than those with a flat top and also shed rain better, thus not corroding as quickly from rust. Because of the extra interior space afforded by the dome shape, these fonts usually had the air chamber inside them, but separated from the fuel below by a metal "floor." Dead-flame lanterns did not have air chambers.

Flat font.

Dome-shaped font.

Air Chamber

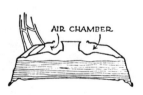

Air chamber in dome-shaped
font of the tubular lantern.

The air chamber was above the font and below the burner. In lanterns with flat fonts, it sat on top of the font as a separate unit soldered to the font. In lanterns with dome-shaped fonts, the air chamber was located inside the dome of the font, above the fuel compartment.

In all these fonts, the air chamber floor prevented fuel from flooding into the burner. A metal wick channel or tube from the burner through the air chamber and opening into the fuel supply in the lower font provided the route for the wick, from fuel to flame.

The main function of the air chamber was to act as the passageway for air — hot or cold (partially burned or fresh) — moving from the side tubes up through the burner mesh to the flame. The size of the air chamber relative to the size of the other lantern parts (e.g., globe, wick, burner, mesh, or globe plate) determined the brightness of the flame. The correct combination produced a steady, bright white (cold-blast) or yellow (hot-blast) flame.

In dead-flame lanterns, there was no air chamber as such. Air was drawn in through holes in the lantern base below the font, straight up into the globe, where it reached the wick and flame.

Burner

The lantern burner functioned as a kind of carburetor, in which vaporized fuel and air (oxygen) were mixed at the flame. The relative proportions of the burner, and of the other lantern parts affected the "mix" which in turn affected the brightness of the flame.

The burner also held the wick in place, and those burners with ratchets allowed easy adjustment of the wick up or down. With earlier, dead-flame lanterns, many burner styles did not have adjusters, and one had to pull the wick up by hand to trim it, or to adjust the flame.

Exterior view of burner, with wick in place.

Various burner styles are illustrated below and on the following pages.

In May of 1857, R. E. Dietz patented a flat-wick burner for coal oil. It was for a dead-flame lantern. Within two years, his brother, Michael Dietz, had patented the improved version shown below in the actual patent forms. These are construction drawings of each part prior to assembly.

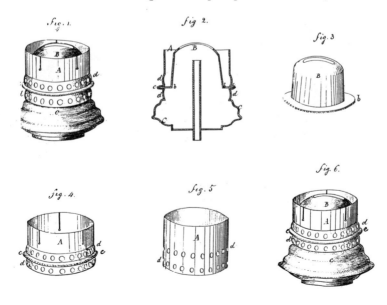

On May 12, 1863, patent 38537 was granted to Timothy J. Dietz for the kerosene burner, shown in the drawings below from the actual patent forms. Also suitable for dead-flame lanterns, this burner closely resembled most of the ones used today. Unlike the one shown on the preceding page, it had a wick adjuster.

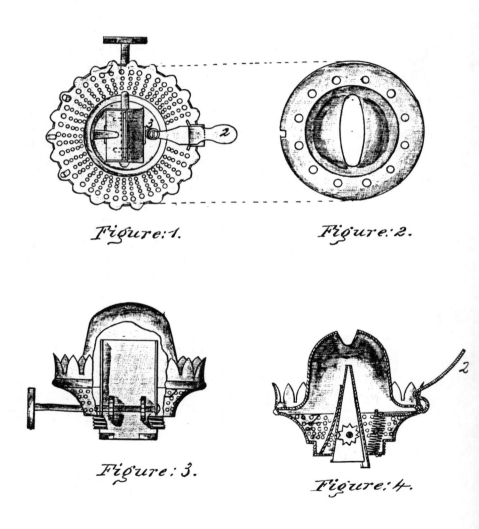

Figure: 1.   Figure: 2.

Figure: 3.   Figure: 4.

Burners for Dead-Flame Lanterns

These early burners, shown below and on the following page were for dead-flame lanterns. The "rope-type" wicks on the earlier ones were not sized and not very economical. The burner with the ratchet adjuster was developed about 1863 but not extensively used until the 1870s, because it was so expensive to manufacture. Refinements in design eventually made it cheaper to produce.

Sperm or Signal Oil
Round Wick 1830 – 1890

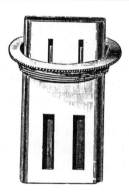 

Sperm or Signal Oil
Flat Wick 1860 – 1890

Sperm or Signal Oil
Burner with Ratchet for Adjusting Wick
1870 – 1910

Minot
1860 – 1890

Signal Oil Flat Wick
1875 – 1925

Minot Heater Burner

The Minot is a burner of unusual design, intended for lanterns burning lard or signal oil. Such fuels solidified in low winter temperatures, making it difficult or impossible to get the lantern to burn steadily. This burner transferred heat from the flame down the tubes to the fuel, softening it.

There were also other burners designed to do this, but they did not have the lower tube and did not work well on very cold days. The use of the Minot died out as better fuels became cheaper and were used more extensively.

Signal Oil Flat Wick

This and similar flat-wick signal oil burners were typical of those used by night watchmen in areas of high fire risk. (They used locked lanterns that could be filled only in appropriate places and at appropriate times. The purpose was to avoid fire when, for instance, a lantern was refilled in the dark and fuel was spilled.) Since the lantern was locked, with the device shown here one could remove the char from the wick without unlocking and opening the lantern. The burner shown was for use on dead-flame lanterns. Hot-blast and cold-blast lanterns used a similar but not identical burner.

Kerosene Burners for Dead-Flame Lanterns
1860 – 1930

The burners shown on the following page, appeared on lanterns as early as 1861. Used with dead-flame lanterns, they were not dependent upon an airtight chimney (or globe) and an air chamber to regulate air to the flame. (The only function of the globe here was to keep out wind and rain.) These burners were forerunners of the hot- and cold-blast lantern burners that closely regulated air flow. Besides the air coming through the bottom-draft holes of the lantern, these burners had a sort of auxiliary air flow channeled around the flame, making it more brilliant. These burners had far less candlepower than the burners in hot- and cold-blast lanterns. They all used flat wicks.

Savage

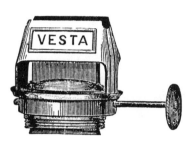

Vesta

Callender

Simplex

Adlake

Convex

Kerosene Burners for Hot- and Cold-Blast Lanterns
1870 – 1945

These burners were dependent on an air-tight globe (chimney) and side tubes for their efficient combustion. Thus, they were part of a semisealed system, with air flow carefully controlled. The air came from the tubes and flowed up through the inside of the burner, as well as through the globe plate holes. These burners all used flat wicks.

Extra air flow

Long cone

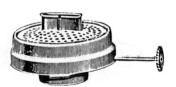

Cone-less

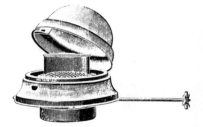

Wire mesh

Burner Styles Typical of Interior Lamps
1870 – 1945

These are shown here because sometimes outdoor lanterns did have this style of burner. They were multipurpose and could be used on dead-flame, hot-blast, or cold-blast lanterns, because they had auxiliary air holes. Like many multipurpose designs, they were not very efficient, but they had their uses. These burners all used flat wicks.

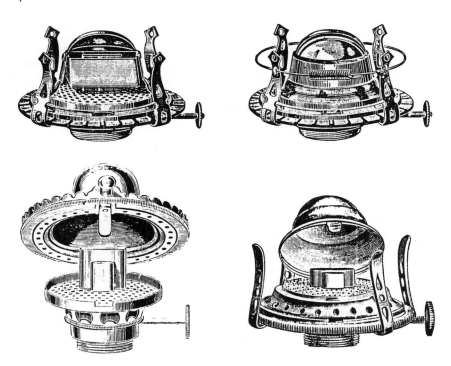

Burner Style for Camphine Lanterns

No 19th-century illustration of a camphine burner has been located, but this rough sketch conveys its distinctive design. Camphine burners are often mistaken for "whale oil" burners, but there was no special design for the latter. Camphine, however, was so explosive that it required its own burner style. It was dangerous even to blow out a camphine-burning burner, as this fuel might spatter and start a fire. Thus, camphine burners came with snuffers attached to them by a chain. The two wicks were high, and separated, to keep the flame away from the volatile fuel in the font. The use of this burner died out as soon as a safer-burning fluid was available at an affordable price.

Side Tubes

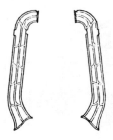

In hot- and cold-blast lanterns, side tubes carried air to the flame. They helped focus a strong draft. If the tubes broke or developed a leak, the lantern ceased to function correctly. Tubes also physically strengthened the lantern. Dead-flame lanterns did not have side tubes. The tubes shown here have the crimp marks characteristic of streamline-style lanterns.

Cross Guards

Lantern cross guards were designed to protect the globe from cracking, breaking, or dislodging. They also served as retaining wires to prevent the globe from falling out of the globe plate when tipped into the open position for cleaning or lighting. There were many styles of globe guards, varying with the lantern date, style, and manufacturer.

Globe Plate

The globe plate in hot- and cold-blast lanterns helped in two ways to assure that only the proper amount of air was fed to the burner. First, because the globe rested on it, the plate was carefully designed, in each lantern model, to prevent air leakage around the under edge of the globe. The weight of the globe helped create the seal. Second, the holes in the plate were not random. Their number and size helped determine the air flow. (Incorrect air flow changed the air-fuel mix, resulting in loss of flame brilliance). Dead-flame lanterns did not have globe plates. The sizing of the holes around their lantern bases helped provide correct air flow, much as did the holes in the globe plate.

Globes

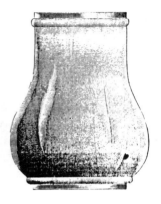

The size and shape of a lantern globe helped determine the amount of air that reached the flame. It was one of the lantern elements, along with wick, burner size, and so on that interacted to produce a bright flame. The globe also protected the flame while still allowing it to be visible. Some globes actually had molded into their glass a lens — the Fresnel or Bull's-eye — which served to intensify or focus the light.

Many of the earliest lamps and lanterns had glass "windows," panes set in the metal frame of the lamp on several sides to protect the flame. Typically, these panes evolved into chimneys, for indoor lamps, and into globes, for outdoor lanterns. At some interim period, there were lanterns that had interior chimneys and "windows" as well. Many street lights of the period exhibited this characteristic.

Another function of the globe was to provide the color needed for various kinds of signal lanterns used on bridges, railroads, carriages, boats, and automobiles.

Globes usually were made for a specific lantern, although similar lanterns were often designed to use the same globe. In an emergency, another globe might fit a lantern other than the one it was designed for. One globe, called a "Fitall" or "Fitzall," was used for this purpose. However, use of a different globe usually sacrificed candlepower; the flame would be less brilliant.

Globe Lift

Lifts made it easier to raise or lower the globe smoothly. Some types, such as the braced lift, were fastened to the globe plate and could lock the globe into the up (open) position while lighting, or the down (closed) position once the flame was lit. This type of lift was braced at an angle betweeen the tube and the font, thereby giving the lantern more rigidity between the side tubes.

The spring lifter, of different design than that shown here (see p. 60), was atop the lantern, below the dome, working from that position to open or close the globe.

Top Dome or Bell

Lantern domes covered the lantern and protected the flame. They helped monitor the amount and velocity of the air that reached the flame. The dome was often the place on the lantern to which the bail was attached or the manufacturer's name was stamped.

Within the dome of a cold-blast lantern, a metal cylinder, resting on the globe, formed a central "chimney" up to the top plate. This separated used air and fresh air when the lantern was burning. Shown by the dotted lines in the drawing, this flue also kept dust and water from the flame. This was particularly important when the lantern was being used in a warehouse or a mine where, say, coal dust was prevalent.

The domes of dead-flame and hot-blast lanterns were simpler. The hot-blast dome separated burned and fresh air only partially; the dead-flame dome did not perform this function at all.

Reflectors and Hoods

Many lanterns had hoods or reflectors that served to shield or reflect and intensify the light from the flame. For example, reflectors could be positioned above the lantern, as with ceiling lights, to reflect the light downward; or behind the lantern, to reflect it forward. Hoods served to keep the light out of the eyes of the lantern user. Reflectors were usually made of silvered glass or of spun, polished

metal. Hoods were made of metal, sometimes painted black outside and white, or unpainted inside. You will see many examples of reflectors and hoods as you look through the illustrations in Section II.

Lantern Materials, Finishes and Markings

Most lantern manufacturers used the same materials, finishes and methods to make their lanterns. Markings, colors and designs of course varied from maker to maker. However, a good design was soon copied, as much as was legally possible, and sometimes, outright, which led to much 19th century patent litigation.

Materials and Manufacturing Methods

Early lantern parts were usually cut from a sheet of mild steel (a soft, malleable steel), of brass or of copper or from some combination of these. For example, the font could be brass and the top steel, or vice versa. Certain kinds of lanterns were sometimes made of heavy (thicker) steel. Rare exceptions are lanterns made wholly or partly of silver or gold.

Once they were cut from the metal sheets, parts were stamped into forms (font, side tubes, bell, etc.) and, where necessary, soldered to keep their shape. All these parts were then soldered into place, piece by piece, to form the lantern. Hard work indeed, for the fumes from the solder vats were overwhelming, and workers could hardly breathe.

All this cutting, stamping, and hand soldering meant that lantern manufacturing was a very labor-intensive business. Nevertheless, lanterns were made this way until well into the 20th century. (One notable exception to this was the "drawn" font of all Dietz lanterns after 1870. Dietz brought a machine from England that was strong enough to "draw" or mold a font out of one piece of metal. A base was soldered onto this piece to make it more stable, but this base did not, as in two-piece fonts, form the font bottom. The two-piece font could leak fuel; the drawn fonts did not.)

It was only with the advent of the "streamlined" lantern models in the 1930s that manufacturing methods changed. Streamlined models were not soldered, but crimped and overlapped by machine. That is, the parts were molded by machine into the correct form, and a seam, or fold, shows along the edges. Crimp marks are also visible on the side tubes, which were crimped to strengthen them, as the metal was very thin. The discovery of such mold marks tells you that the lantern in question is not an early model, even though its style appears to date from the 19th century.

Making lanterns by hand seems even harder when one considers how many times there were design changes, even of small parts, which necessitated changing the dies or templates. Of course, by retaining this method of soldering together individual parts, such hand-done methods facilitated retooling. In the 19th century, new manufacturers' catalogs, where all the new designs or refinements were listed, appeared every few years. By the 20th century, new catalogs were coming out perhaps only once in a decade, because designs were relatively standardized by then and because the market had narrowed considerably.

Globes

Lantern globes were usually contracted out to glass manufacturers, rather than being made by the lantern company. Such manufacturers were legion and made many globe styles. (For example, in 1896 the Macbeth Glass Company in Pittsburgh offered 1,350 different styles of chimneys and globes for lamps and lanterns. In 1914, Dietz bought and shipped, with its lanterns, three million globes.)

Globes were either clear or colored, depending upon their intended use. The colored ones came in two kinds; *genuine* and *imitation* (sprayed on or fire baked on). Those of *genuine* color had the coloring material mixed in with the molten glass before being molded. They were the more expensive, for the color never diminished, continuing to give good visibility. (Remember that the color was to be seen, not to see with. These globes were still brilliant at a distance.)

Imitation-color globes were clear globes sprayed with colored lacquers. They were more visible than those of *genuine* or fire-baked color. However, their durability was poor; the color wore off. The fire-baked types were clear globes covered with a colored paste, which was baked onto the globe. These globes were so dark that it was difficult to see the light through them, and they tended to have the poorest visibility from a distance. Color was also added to some lanterns by the means of variously colored glass panes, which were slipped over a part of the globe or lens.

Finishes

Once molded or soldered, lanterns were "finished" in various ways. The finish served to prevent or retard rusting and, in the case of paint, to help identify the lanterns. All these finishes gave roughly equal protection.

Typically, mild-steel lanterns were finished by most manufacturers in bright tin, nickel plate, copperplate, brass plate, bronze, clear lacquer, japan, or paint. If a lantern was made of brass or copper sheet, its finish usually was nickel plate, japan, clear lacquer, paint, or natural polish. Lanterns made of a combination of steel parts and brass or copper parts were often finished as though the whole lantern were made of mild steel.

Experience will train you to recognize the subtle differences in appearance of some of these finishes, so keep looking and continue to make comparisons among the different lanterns you come across. It is difficult to convey these differences in words, but here are some examples.

- **Bronze finish** was yellow to olive-brown in color. It looks different from brass; although it, too is very shiny, it looks browner.

- **Bright tin** is duller-looking than **nickel plate,** which is very shiny. However, both these finishes were, in earlier lanterns, obtained by *dipping* the lantern in these substances. After about 1900, however, the same finishes were achieved through *electroplating.* The electroplated finish looks shinier than the dipped finish but lacks the depth of color; it is thinner.

- **Lacquered** lanterns can be distinguished by their lack of tarnish or rust. They look clearer and brighter than the natural material. However, lacquer can fade to a dull, yellow tint. It may peel or flake off in less protected areas of the lantern. Note also that only ferrous metal (mild steel) rusts; brass gets brittle and may crack or corrode.

- **Japan,** an oriental enamel, yielded a finish less thick-looking than that produced by the regular paint, a durable, high-gloss enamel. Both japan and paint came in several colors, some of which served to identify the lantern owners. For example, in the same town the water department might have had its lanterns painted blue and the highway department have had its painted yellow. Then, anyone who came to a work site to collect the lanterns knew which ones belonged to his department.

Markings

Typically, a lantern is marked with the manufacturer's name, a patent date, and, sometimes, the lantern style, but there were sometimes other markings. Markings served to show ownership, the lantern type, the maker's name, and the patent numbers. Ownership markings were a protection against theft, and many large users of lanterns required that their names be stamped indelibly in a prominent place on the lantern during the manufacturing process. Usually, such lettering is impressed into the metal just above the globe, where it is clearly visible. Stamping below, on the font, was less effective, since the markings would be obscured by the oily dirt that collected there, or hidden, when the font was buried in earth or sand to keep the lantern from blowing over.

The *manufacturer's name* almost always was stamped on a lantern, usually on the top (bell) or the font. The style of lantern was another common stamping, (e.g., No. 39). If the manufacturer's name was on the lantern, the style was usually there too. After 1940, Dietz streamlined lanterns had the *font size* number stamped on the font. Other markings typical of a specific manufacturer are noted, along with their positions, where known, in Section II, under each manufacturer.

Ownership marking

Less frequently, the *patent date* was imprinted, usually on the top or the side tubes. This practice was fairly common until about the mid-1930s, but less so thereafter. It may be that the designs were obsolete or that the patents were beginning to run out just as the market for lanterns was dwindling. Thus, manufacturers did not bother to renew.

Although many of the illustrations in this book show lantern globes with extensive markings molded or etched into their glass, most globes did not actually look like this. These pictures, with their markings, were used for advertising purposes to stress the name of a lantern, the fact that it was patented, the manufacturer's name, or some particular feature of the product. If a globe was marked, it usually was with letters much smaller than those in the illustrations. You may have to search for them.

A marking you may come across on some Dietz lanterns is illustrated below. This is Hindi for "Real Dietz. Made in America." It was stamped onto the font of lanterns made for sale in India. Those found in the United States are probably overruns from such Indian sales contracts.

अमेरिका

आसलिंडाट्ज़ुज़, निमाद

Locations of patent dates.

Lantern Fuels: Then and Now

Lantern fuels reflected and followed the course of American enterprise and technology. From lard oil to today's kerosene, the wicks, fonts, burners, and general construction of lanterns all were adapted to utilize each new fuel.

These changes were not, of course, always immediate. The use of some of the older fuels, and the lanterns designed for them, persisted for a time, depending upon local availability and their relative cost, efficiency, and safety. Thus, there are numerous overlaps in the chronology of lantern fuels, and many lanterns were designed with interchangeable wicks and burners, or ones that would burn several fuels. Rural regions were then, as they are today, slower than urban areas to pick up newer or more expensive technologies. Regional and other differences affected use as well.

During the earlier and middle parts of the 19th century, there were more rapid and fundamental changes in fuels than in lantern design. The earlier fuels tended to be expensive, or unsafe, or inefficient, and the emphasis was on finding a better fuel. With the advent of kerosene, which was cheaper, or safer, or more efficient than other fuels in its production of light, the emphasis changed to designing lanterns that better utilized this fuel.

Broadly speaking, the dates of the popular use of the different lantern fuel oils are as follows:

Lard Oil: early settlers to the 1880s

Whale Oil: 1820s until about 1910

Camphine: 1850 to the 1860s

Burning Fluid: 1845 to the 1870s

Coal Oil: 1856 well into the 1860s

Petroleum: 1859 to the 1870s (the petroleum we use
              today is a different compound)

Kerosene: 1856 to the present day (in a more refined
              form)

Signal Oil: 1860 to the early 1920s

Lard Oil

Lard oil was rendered animal fat, (i.e., boiled pig, raccoon, possum, or whatever passed by). This fuel was particularly common in rural areas, because it was cheap and available. The railroads used it for the same reasons, long after other fuels were more widely used. This fuel did not burn as brightly as some of the later ones. What was more of a flaw, it congealed as it got colder, making it difficult to get the lantern to burn. (It also turned rancid as the weather got warmer, and must have smelled rather bad.) Several burners, including the Minot, were designed that partly overcame this problem (see p. 18). Many of the early dead-flame lanterns burned lard oil, so its use persisted until late into the 19th century in many areas.

Whale Oil

Whale oil was, of course, more available and cheaper in or near the coastal regions than in the interior. Several kinds of whale oil were used as fuel, but it was oil from the sperm whale that gave the brightest and cleanest flame. Increased supplies of whale oil in the industrial East stimulated improved design of lantern oil reservoirs and wicks. The use of whale oil began to decrease by the 1880s and died out soon after the turn of the century.

Camphine

Camphine was patented by a Mr. Webb in 1839 but was not widely available until about 1850. Camphine is an oil, or distilled oil, of turpentine, obtained from pine trees. Highly explosive and unstable, it caused fires in more homes and factories than did any other fuel. Nevertheless, it had two advantages. The cost was approximately one-third that of whale oil, which retailed at about $2.00 a gallon when it was first marketed. Second, it burned with a brighter light. Thus, it was used in spite of its riskiness. Because of its volatility, camphine had some impact on lantern design. Often mistaken for a "whale oil" burner, its distinctive burner and

Downer's Mineral Sperm Oil

USED WITH THE TUBULAR LANTERN, IS AS SAFE AS

SPERM OR WHALE OIL.

CERTIFICATE.

NEW YORK, September 15, 1870.

J. TRUMBULL SMITH, ESQ.,

MANAGER OF THE AMERICAN INSTITUTE FAIR.

Dear Sir:—Having been informed that there has been some objections to the burning of "Downer's Mineral Sperm" in the Fair, on account of the supposed danger from fire, I would respectfully say that I have used and tested the "Mineral Sperm Oil," and that I consider it safer than any other hydro-carbon oil in use at the present time, and fully as safe as sperm oil. It stands a flashing test of 250 degrees, F., and a burning test of 292 degrees, F. The legal standard is, flashing point, 100 degrees, F., and burning point, 110 degrees, F. As my experiments on (24) twenty-four different lamps showed that the temperature of the oil never rises in practice above 100 degrees, F., which is 150 degrees below the flashing, and 192 degrees below the burning point of the "Mineral Sperm," I have just grounds for saying this oil is as safe as sperm whale oil.

Respectfully yours.

C. F. CHANDLER,

Prof. of Chemistry, Columbia College and School of Mines.

This advertisement, for what appears to be a mixture of camphine and some other oil, is addressed to the public's fears about the safety of camphine oil as a lighting fluid.

wick are illustrated on page 21. Glass fonts were also designed for camphine-burning lanterns, since the fuel got so hot in metal fonts that there was danger of fire from its igniting.

During the Civil War, the price of camphine rose to $5.00 a gallon, and it eventually was priced out of the market. In addition, the war brought advances in lighting technology, and by the end of the war, kerosene was beginning to replace camphine.

Burning Fluid

Burning fluid was discovered by a Mr. Jennings about 1834. He called it spirit gas. Popular by the 1840s, this mixture of turpentine and alcohol was used in lanterns without chimneys. Very volatile, it burned with a pure white light. Jennings invented a burner for this fuel. However, its use was relatively short-lived, because of the coming of kerosene.

Coal Oil

Coal oil was discovered in the 1840s and appeared on the market in salable quantities about 1856. Originally distilled from coal shale materials in Scotland, it was first made in the New World in Nova Scotia, by the distillation of a bituminous, asphalt-like material, albertine. Later, grahamite, a black, lustrous asphaltite found in West Virginia and Kentucky, was distilled to produce coal oil. While this compound resembled kerosene as we know it today, it was not quite as refined. Used widely for about a decade, coal oil was efficient, safer than camphine, and cheaper than whale oil. Its distillation was a slow process, however, and was dropped with the discovery of crude oil, which was more efficiently and quickly processed.

Petroleum

What we are here calling petroleum, also known as rock oil, or crude oil, is not the same compound as modern-day petroleum. (**Do not try to use the latter in your lanterns!**) Earlier in the century, it was used in New York State, near the Pennsylvania border, where it seeped out of the ground naturally. It even was used as a medicine, the legendary cure-all, "snake oil." The first oil well in the United States was drilled in Venango County, Pennsylvania, where Colonel Edward Drake struck oil in August 1859. Petroleum displaced coal oil as a lantern fuel, and in turn was displaced by kerosene. A different form of petroleum continues to be used today in a variety of ways, above all as an automobile fuel.

Kerosene

Kerosene is a distillate of coal oil, petroleum, rock oil, or crude oil. Widely available by the late 1850s, it was efficient, very stable, and economical. It stimulated more new lantern designs than any other fuel. It continues in use, although today's kerosene is a more refined version of the 19th century compound.

Signal Oil

Signal oil is a heavy-grade oil, a mixture of kerosene and lard oil, sperm oil, or vegetable oil. If not mixed properly, it will cause the lantern wick to char too frequently during burning. Differently proportioned mixtures are used during summer and winter because, like lard oil, signal oil congeals at lower temperatures. It was used by steamship and railroad companies well into the 1920s, but during the First World War the government had asked railroads to stop using lard oil as a fuel. (By that time, it consisted of about 40 per cent hog fat, which the Allies and the United States needed for munitions manufacture.) Lack of lard oil led to the end of signal oil, as railroads began moving to kerosene.

Today, the fuels used in American lanterns are kerosene (in its contemporary form) and various "lantern fuels," often scented, sold for use in some modern imitations of old lanterns. All these can be used in older restored lanterns as well.

Section II:
Major American Manufacturers and Their Lanterns:

Illustrations, Specifications, Uses, Comparative Rarity

Although many companies made or sold one or more types of lanterns during the 19th century, this does not mean that the collector will be able to find many kinds of lanterns from each different manufacturer. Many types are very rare, as lanterns often were only one line of hardware products among many put out by such companies. Moreover, the earliest 19th-century lantern manufacturers made very few kinds of lanterns. Styles had not yet been modified or new designs developed, nor was there as much competition and, therefore, the need to carry and sell a broad product line.

As lantern demand increased and design improved, competition became fierce. Businesses came and went; some failed, some were sued for patent violations, and some were bought out. By the late 1800s, many companies were so short-lived that they produced few lanterns or any other product. Consequently, it would be a singular find if you came across a lantern from one of the companies whose output was small or short-lived, or limited to the earlier part of the century. Most of the older lanterns still around are — not always, but usually — the few survivors of a larger original output.

The companies dealt with in this book are those that were significant manufacturers of lanterns — significant because lanterns were among their major or perhaps only products. They were in business for an extended period of time or were bought out by another lantern company, which may have continued manufacturing some of their lanterns. These are the companies whose lanterns you are most likely to come across, whether rarely or commonly, and will wish to identify, repair, or restore.

The most conspicuous among such companies is Dietz, which in 1990 celebrated 150 years of lamp and lantern making. Adams and Westlake (or Adlake) is another of the old lantern companies still in business, although it no longer makes lanterns. These and other significant companies are listed below, chronologically and with notes that clarify the various business maneuvers that took place as companies were bought and sold and patent rights vied for. In the pages that follow, lanterns from these companies are illustrated and original specifications given where available.

After the chronological enumeration comes a listing of some other companies that made lanterns, perhaps briefly or as part of a larger line of products. Little information is available on these companies, and the author has to date found no original illustrations or specifications on their lanterns.

The many other lantern/hardware companies are not included as the purpose of the book is to identify and describe lanterns, not to catalog companies whose product line is relatively or completely unknown and cannot be illustrated here. For a broader company listing, consult the bibliography. (If you do have the unusual good luck to find an early, rare lantern not illustrated here, you can still learn about and restore it using the material in Sections I and III.)

Index to Manufacturers

Archer, Pancoast and Co.	1856 - 1868	Bought by Dietz in 1868.
Dietz and Smith	1868 - 1869	Partnership dissolved after one year.
R. E. Dietz Co.	1869 - present.	Still in business.
Kelly Lamp Co.	1856 - 1897	Apparently went out of business. From about 1889 to 1920, Kelly's son ran the Rochester Headlight Works.
F. Mayrose and Co.	1866 - 1903	Sued by Dietz for patent violations; later went out of business.
Chicago Manufacturing Co.	1868 - 1873	Bought by Dennis and Wheeler.
Dennis and Wheeler	1867 - 1881	Bought by a combine that then founded the Steam Gauge and Lantern Company.
D. D. Miller	1870 - 1920s	Apparently went out of business.
Nail City Lantern Co./ Wheeling Stamping Co.	1877 - present	The Lantern Division of Wheeling Stamping was bought by Dietz in 1946.
Steam Gauge and Lantern Co.	1881 - 1897	Bought by Dietz.
C. T. Ham Manufacturing Co.	1887 - 1914	Almost merged with Dietz but did not; later went out of business.
Defiance Lantern and Stamping Company	1900 - 1935	Bought by Embury Manufacturing.
Embury Manufacturing Co.	1917 - 1953	Bought by Dietz.
Armspear Manufacturing Co./ Railroad Signal Lamp and Lantern Company	1877 - 1940s	Dietz made one attempt to buy but didn't follow through; later went out of business.
Adams and Westlake Limited (Adlake)	1857 - present	Still in business.
Lovell-Dressel Co.	Prior to 1900 to 1968	Bought by Adlake.

Other lantern manufacturers include the following:

Buhl Stamping Company

Ohio Lantern Company

Winfield Manufacturing Company

Berger Manufacturing Company

Bellair Stamping Company

R.A.V. Manufacturing Company*

Howard & Morse*

St.Louis RailroadCompany*

Erwin & Bill Company*

Fullett Lantern Company*

Underhill Lantern Company*

Perko or Perkins Marine Lamp &
Hardware Company,
Brooklyn, New York

Osborn & Company*

Richard Strong Company,
Rochester, New York

Bridgeport Brass Company*

The Porter Company,
New York, New York

The Standard Lantern Company,
Troy, New York

Universal Metal Spinning & Stamping Company, New York, New York

St. Louis Tallin Company

Rayo Manufacturing Company

Star Headlight & Lantern Company,
Rochester, New York

Hanlon Lantern Company

*   The companies marked with an asterisk (*) had patent-violation suits brought against them for copying the hot-blast lantern. Any hot-blast lanterns stamped with these company names will be very rare. In general, lanterns from any of the companies on this list will be rare.

The following pages give details on manufacturers, and all available information to date on markings, specifications, finish, appearance and use. In some instances original language is included from old sales catalogs to convey the flavor of the initial offering. This material is in quotation marks to distinguish it from the regular text.

Archer, Pancoast and Company

Archer, Pancoast was founded in 1856. Located at 9-11 Mercer Street in New York City, it manufactured the then new hot-blast lanterns under license from John Irwin, who held the patent. One of its salesmen, A. G. Smith, had obtained from Irwin the sole right to manufacture and market this hot-blast lantern in the midwestern and eastern United States. For unknown reasons, Archer, Pancoast had by the spring of 1868 gone into bankruptcy. On August 1, Smith formed a partnership with Robert Edwin Dietz, apparently bringing the patent rights with him. Also on August 1, the receiver in the Archer, Pancoast bankruptcy sold to Dietz and Smith the business, tools, and equipment.

Although the Archer, Pancoast line was discontinued in 1868 because of the buyout, the 1869 Dietz and Smith line was very similar, probably because Dietz and Smith was using the Archer, Pancoast molds but marking the lanterns with the Dietz and Smith logo. R. E. Dietz later also manufactured lanterns similar to some of this line, but with different model numbers.

No catalog or sales material has been found for Archer, Pancoast except for one illustrated product list, which is now so deteriorated as to be unprintable. From this list, it appears that the company sold the lanterns listed below. To give some idea of the appearance of Archer, Pancoast lanterns, comparisons are made, where known, to other lanterns illustrated in this book.

– No. 5 Vesta. Similar to the No. 6 Dietz, but smaller.

– No. 2 and No. 8 Champion. Similar to the No. 9 Dietz.

– Convex Reflector, also known as Excelsior Hand Lantern. Similar to the Dietz Convex Reflector except for its oval, rather than square, side reflectors.

– Nonpareil. Similar to the Dietz, but burned sperm oil only.

– Light House. No comparative information.

– No. 0 Tubular Lantern. Similar to the Dietz No. 0 Tubular.

– Illuminator. No comparative information.

Some Archer, Pancoast "logo" stamps for imprinting their lanterns were found in the Dietz archives, presumably part of the equipment that came with the sale to Dietz and Smith. From these it appears that their lanterns were marked with "A & P Co." and the lantern style or type (e.g., "A & P Co. No. 5", or "A & P Co. Excelsior"). It is very rare to find these lanterns.

Dietz and Smith

Dietz and Smith was founded in August 1868, a month before Robert Edwin Dietz left Dietz Brothers and Company, lamp manufacturers. This new partnership was located at 4 College Place at Robinson Street in New York City. The partnership lasted one year, until August 1, 1869, when it was dissolved.

Smith appears to have been an "idea" man with no business sense. According to R. E. Dietz's diary, the first year's sales for Dietz and Smith were less than 500 dozen lanterns, bringing in just enough cash to pay creditors and meet the payroll. Nevertheless, Smith removed all the capital he had put into the company, in order to cover his living expenses. Moreover, at this inopportune moment, he decided that velocipedes (bicycles) were the wave of the future and used $5,000 of company money to stock them. He was too far ahead of his time, and the venture was not the success he had expected. Dietz concluded that Smith was "a dangerous man to do business with" and, after getting an injunction, eventually bought out Smith, and his Irwin patent rights, with some cash and some notes.

A review of various sales records and correspondence indicates that the lantern styles sold by Dietz and Smith, in toto, were those listed below. As we noted before, this line is similar to Archer, Pancoast's and may have been made, this first year after the sale, by using its molds. They were marked "Dietz and Smith" and are now very rare. To give some idea of their appearance, reference is made, where the information is known, to Dietz lamps similar in appearance.

– No. 5 Vesta. Similar to the No. 6 Dietz, but smaller.

– No. 2 Champion. Similar to the No. 9, but smaller.

– Convex Reflector. Similar to the Dietz Convex Reflector Lantern.

– Nonpareil Lantern. Similar to the Dietz Nonpareil.

– No. 1 and No. 0 Tubular Lanterns. Similar to the Dietz No. 1 and No. 0 Tubulars.

This appears to be the only original advertisement from Dietz and Smith remaining in the Dietz archives.

R. E. Dietz Company

R. E. Dietz, as we noted earlier, was originally a partner with his brother in Dietz Brothers and Company. Their major product was a line of very fine interior lamps and girandoles — highly decorated, ornate candelabras. This factory was located at 132-134 Williams Street in New York City. The building burned down on Washington's birthday in 1871, and the company never went back into business.

After R. E. Dietz dissolved his partnership in Dietz and Smith, he continued doing business, under the name R. E. Dietz, at the Dietz and Smith location. He remained there until 1871, when the building was condemned, literally to be cut in half, in order to widen Robinson Street. In the same year, the second R. E. Dietz factory was opened at Fulton and Cliff streets in New York City, remaining in operation until 1887. In that year, the third factory was opened, on Laight Street in Greenwich Village, New York City. Destroyed by fire in June 1897, it was rebuilt in 1898 and used until 1950. A fourth factory was bought from the Steam Gauge and Lantern Company, in July 1897, in Syracuse, New York. It operated concurrently with the New York City factory and is still in operation. Dietz continued to manufacture as R. E. Dietz until 1886, when the company became a New York State corporation, the R. E. Dietz Company. It is now the oldest family-owned company still operating in the state.

Dietz was a good manager and also saw the value of research and development. The latter produced some significant changes in burner design that vastly improved the company's lanterns. Another strength was the acquisition of the Irwin patent rights to the East Coast and the Midwest, through the Archer Pancoast buyout. In 1897, the West Coast rights were obtained as well, through the buyout of the Steam Gauge and Lantern Company of Rochester, New York. Indeed, between 1870 and 1960, R. E. Dietz Company acquired the lantern divisions of almost all the American manufacturers with whom they were in competition.

1914

THE DIETZ LANTERN FACTORIES OF TO-DAY—LARGEST IN THE WORLD

AT SYRACUSE, NEW YORK—OVER 124,000 SQUARE FEET   AT NEW YORK CITY—OVER 84,000 SQUARE FEET

THE expansion of the Tubular Lantern business from three floors to present acreage is strikingly shown in the perspective view of our New York City and Syracuse buildings, combined in the above illustration.

THE DIETZ LANTERN FACTORY at Syracuse, N. Y., is located on Wilkinson Street, opposite Leavenworth Park, about 5 minutes walk from the New York Central Station. The 5 story main building is of mill construction, and is 260 feet long. Every modern device is employed to safeguard the employees and facilitate production.

THE DIETZ FACTORY in New York City is located in the nine-story and basement fire-proof Dietz Building, Greenwich at Laight Street, a short distance from Desbrosses Street Ferry. Here are made in addition to lanterns the Famous Dietz Motor Car Lamps, and the tinned steel burners used in Dietz Lanterns.

THE GENERAL OFFICES OF THE COMPANY ARE IN THE NEW YORK CITY BUILDING, GREENWICH AT LAIGHT ST.

For all of these reasons, Dietz became the largest manufacturer of lanterns in the world.

To facilitate midwestern sales, an office was in 1882 opened at 25 Lake Street, Chicago. Overseas offices were by 1913 in place in: Hamburg, Germany; London, England; Calcutta, India; Bombay, India; Java; Sydney, New South Wales; Buenos Aires, Argentina; Valparaiso, Chile; Barranquilla, Columbia; Mexico City, Mexico; Havana, Cuba; St. Johns, Newfoundland; San Juan, Puerto Rico; Vancouver, British Columbia; the Philippines; the Straits Settlements; Sumatra; Ceylon; Korea; and China. Many of these were closed during World War I because of a scarcity of materials.

In 1955, government regulations barred kerosene lanterns from further use on highways. As a result, Dietz's American sales, which, like those of most lantern companies, were slowing because of the declining use of lanterns, dropped to an all-time low. To counteract this, a subsidiary, R. E. Dietz Limited, was in 1956 set up in Hong Kong to increase Dietz lighting sales in foreign markets and to lower production costs. Lantern production has always been labor-intensive. By moving all lantern production overseas, where labor is relatively cheap, Dietz could improve its competitive position.

Nine tubular lantern models are currently in production in the Hong Kong factory. The R. E. Dietz Company in Syracuse, New York, imports only three of these for United States distribution: the Little Wizard, the Air Pilot, and the Original. All nine of the Hong Kong lanterns are sold to overseas markets around the world.

Today the Dietz factories in Syracuse manufacture automotive lighting equipment, primarily for commercial equipment: trucks, tractor trailers, snowplows, and emergency vehicles, such as police cars and ambulances. Battery-operated flashers for mounting on construction barricades also are part of their line.

Dietz lanterns are marked with the name of the manufacturer and the type (e.g., "Dietz Hy-lo," "Dietz O Tubular," "Dietz 30," and "Dietz Ironclad"). The markings are on the font or on the top (bell), depending on the lantern style or type.

After 1940, some streamline-style lanterns had font size numbers (e.g., "No. 1" through "No. 8,") stamped on the font in large writing. These should not be confused with the model number. Displaying the font size number was a sales idea intended to emphasize to the customer the lantern's oil capacity rather than, as in the past, its burning time.

From the 1880s to the 1930s, Dietz manufactured special-order one-of-a-kind lanterns. These were usually made as gifts for 30- and 40-year railroad employees. Probably only a few hundred were ever made. Usually gold- or silver-plated, or even solid gold or silver, of railroad lantern style, they were marked "Dietz." Such one-of-a-kind lanterns are not shown in the listings that follow, but you may recognize them by their unusual materials and attractiveness. For instance, the American Museum of Fire Fighting in Hudson, New York, has a magnificent gold-plated D-Lite Lantern, which had been presented to a fire company. It is slightly wider than the normal D-Lite.

Nonpareil Lantern
1869 – 1875.

6" x 8" side windows; available with clear, red, or green glass.
Dead flame.

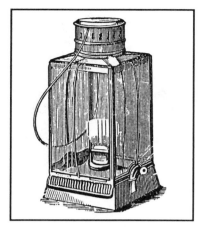

Like many early lanterns, it was adaptable, having a sperm oil burner and candle socket as well as a kerosene burner. It was advertised as a cheap lantern for farm and general use, and sales records indicate it also was used extensively on canals, with colored glasses, as a signal light.

Very rare.

Convex Reflector Lantern
1869 – 1875.

A small lantern with a convex reflector and a hinged bottom. Its side windows were cut from 7" x 9" window glass.
Burned kerosene.
Dead flame.

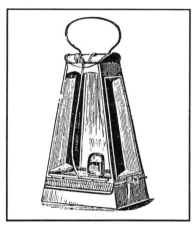

This type and style of lantern was sold by many other lantern companies, as well. Hardware stores and feed stores carried it as early as 1858, sales being particularly directed toward midwestern farmers.

Very rare.

No. 13 Satellite Lantern
1870 – 1874.

Dead flame.

Note in the quotation that the term used is neither "globe" nor "chimney", but rather "glass." In 1874 replacement glasses cost $1.00 each, which was expensive.
For use in and around the home.

Very rare.

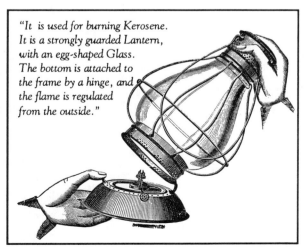

"It is used for burning Kerosene. It is a strongly guarded Lantern, with an egg-shaped Glass. The bottom is attached to the frame by a hinge, and the flame is regulated from the outside."

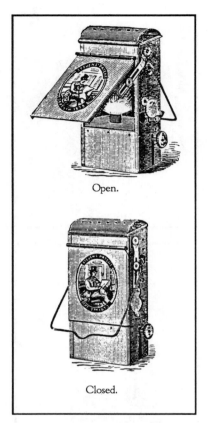

Open.

Closed.

Stevens Patent Pocket Lantern
1878 – 1897.

5 1/2" high, 2 1/2" wide, and 1 1/2" thick.
No. O burner, 3/8" wick.
Dead flame.
Decorated tin, with a colored design.

Used by amateur photographers as a primitive flash. The lid, usually closed, was opened to expose film and then closed again. This is not marked "Dietz" and may have been made under license to Stevens, who designed this lantern.

Rare.

Farm Lantern
1880 – 1897.

Three windows each 7" x 9".
It came with an oil burner for sperm oil, a candle socket, and a nonadjustable kerosene burner. Dead flame.

Before 1888, the Dietz sales department often was instructed to sell this lantern at 20 percent below wholesale. This was unusual, perhaps indicating that Dietz did not manufacture it. After 1888 this lantern was marked **"New Farm Lantern"** and came only with an adjustable kerosene burner. It is almost impossible to find the earlier model with all three inserts.

Very rare: both models.

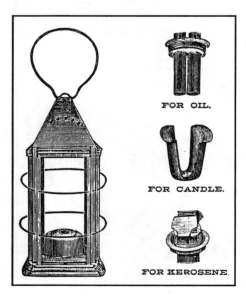

FOR OIL.

FOR CANDLE.

FOR KEROSENE.

No. 15 Tubular Side Lantern
1873 – 1906.

Weight: 1.3 lbs.
"A" burner (later became the "No. 1");
5/8" wick.
No. O Tubular Globe.
Finish: Bright tin or bronzed. After 1890,
japanned blue was offered instead of bronze.
Hot blast.

In 1875, a 6" glass reflector was added.
The side mount was used to fasten the
lantern to a wall.

Rare.

"It gives the same amount of light as the No. 1
Tubular Lantern, and is intended for house or
outside use. This Side Lamp is the leading size.
Cannot explode. No Smoke or Smell. No
heated Globes to break. Can be lighted and
regulated without removing the Globe."

No. 16 Tubular Side Lamp
1873 – 1874.

Weight: 1.9 lbs.
"B" burner (later became the "No. 2");
1" wick.
No. 1 Tubular Globe.
Hot blast.
Finish: bright tin.

An intermediate size between the No. 15
and No. 17, it may not have been much
in demand, which could account for its
short production period.

Very rare.

"Currents of wind do not interfere with its
burning. These Side Lamps are the best and
safest light for Factories, Stables, or any place
where a stationary light is required. Can be light-
ed and regulated without removing the Globe."

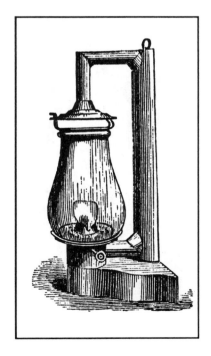

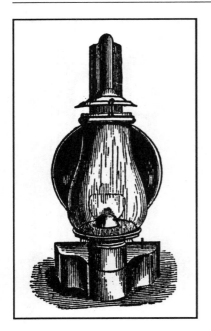

No. 17 Tubular Side Lamp
1873 – 1906.

Weight: 2.6 lbs.; 1" burner;
6" glass reflector.
Hot blast.
Finish: bright tin or bronzed, 1873 – 1890;
thereafter japanned blue only.

Sold as an indoor wall or stand-up lamp.

Rare.

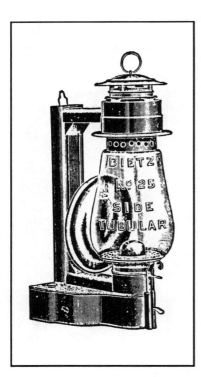

No. 25 Tubular Side Lamp
1894 – 1914.

Height: 15"; 1" wick; 30 candlepower.
Cold blast.
Finish: japanned blue.

Common.

No. 15 Tubular Side Lamp
(not shown)
1894 – 1925.

Height: 15"; 5/8" wick; 20 candlepower.
Cold blast.
Finish: japanned blue.

Similar style to No. 25.

About this time lantern specifications generally began to include light output, that is, the amount of candlepower. Perhaps this had become a selling point.

Common.

No. 30 Beacon Lantern
1913 – 1945.

Height: 15 1/4"; 1" wick; 50 candlepower.
Spun metal reflector, 12" front diameter,
7" deep. A 2 3/4" bull's eye lens was an
option. It focused the light and made it
stronger.
Cold blast
Finish: japanned blue.

Common.

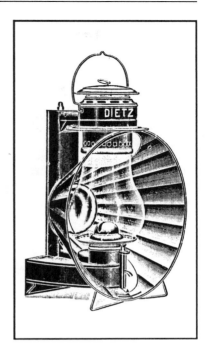

No. 60 Beacon Lantern
1913 – 1930.

Height: 20 1/2"; 1 1/2" wick;
100 candlepower.

Spun metal reflector, 16" diameter,
5" back, and 10" deep.
Cold blast.
Finish: japanned blue.

Rare.

These lanterns were used in mills,
warehouses, workshops, stables, and
summer resorts.

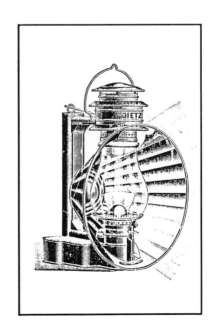

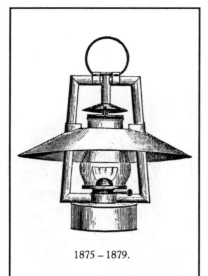

1875 – 1879.

1880 – 1887.

No. 2 Tubular Reflector Lantern
1875 – 1892.

No. 2 burner, 1" wick.
Hot blast.

In 1880, the bail clamps were strengthened; the font base was enlarged so that the lantern was less likely to tip over. In 1888, wire guard protection was added to the globe; tubes were curved, and stamping appeared on the reflector. Over the years the style of this lamp changed as shown.

This lantern was intended for use in mines.

Very rare: 1875 – 1887 models

Rare: 1888 – 1892 model

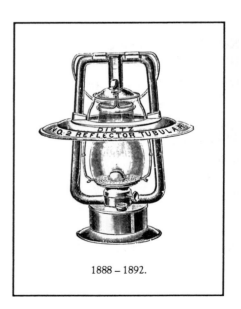

1888 – 1892.

Blizzard No. 1 or No. 2 or
No. 1 or No. 2 Tubular Lantern
1898 – 1912.

Height: No. 1, 13 3/4".
Height: No. 2, 15".
The crank to raise the globe is on the outside of the side tubes. This distinguishes it from the Blizzard No.1 or No. 2 shown next. Cold blast.
Finish: Bright tin; bright tin with copper font; bright tin, copper-plated and polished, with copper font.

This lantern was sold as a reflector (directing light downward) lantern for mills, mines, storehouses, and factories. It can be found with any of the above names stamped on it.

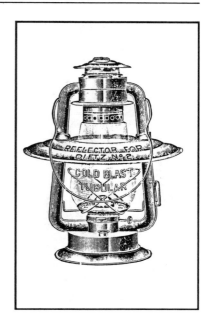

No. 1 was a poor seller and after a few years, orders for it were filled with the No. 2 lantern, probably because it gave a brighter light thanks to its larger size.

Rare.

Very rare with copper font, or with reflector still in place.

No. 1 Blizzard Lantern
1912 – 1938.

Height: 13 3/4"; 5/8" wick; 6 candlepower.
Cold blast.

This was not as good a sales item as the No. 2, which offered many font sizes.

Rare.

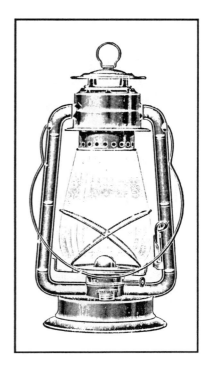

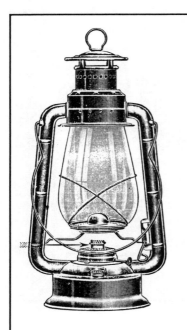

1912 – 1945.

1939 – 1960s.

No. 2 Blizzard Lantern
1912 – 1945.

Height: 15"
Cone-less burner. (see p. 20),
1" wick; 10 candlepower.
Cold blast.
Finish: bright tin; between 1912 and 1920,
bright tin with brass fonts or bright tin with
brass font and brass top.

Made with font sizes allowing from 18 to 60 hours burning time. Also available with 100-hour, square font, enameled red. The cone was manufactured as part of the globe plate, instead of separately, so it could not be lost. (See Simplex Lantern, p. 59.) In 1939 an attempt to reintroduce a brass font was unsuccessful.

These were popular highway lanterns into the 1930s and 1940s; an absolutely wind and weatherproof source of light, without electricity. Red globes are common.

Common: tin.

Rare: other styles.

No. 2 Blizzard Lantern
1939 – 1960s.

Streamlined version of the 1912 – 1945
lantern.
Cold blast.
Finish: iridescent blue paint.

Very common.

No. 2 Simplex Lantern
1910 – 1915.

Height: 13 1/2"
"Cone-less" burner; 1" wick;
5 candlepower.
Hot blast.
Finish: bright tin only.

This was a round side-tube version of the "OK" lantern (see p. 66.)

Rare.

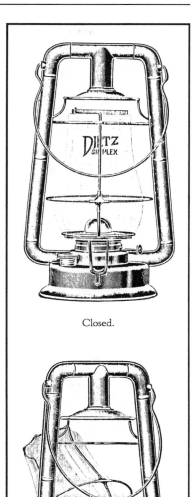

Closed.

Open, showing exposed wick tube
and "cone-less" burner.

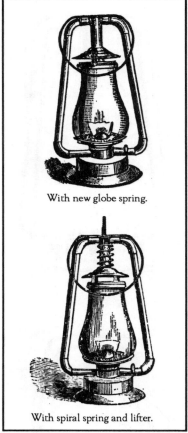

With new globe spring.

With spiral spring and lifter.

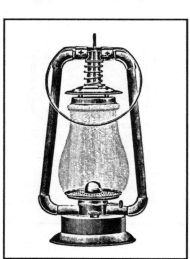

No. O Tubular Lantern
1870 – 1884.

No. O Burner, 3/8" wick.
Clear, ruby, green, and blue globes.
Hot blast.
Finish: bright tin.

This was one of the first hot-blast lanterns and helped account for Dietz's great increase in sales, from 6,000 in 1869 to 1,600,000 between 1870 to 1874.

After 1875 the spring lifter was no longer used and side tubes no longer had corner braces. The more expensive model had a spring lifter, which made it easy to open and also kept it tightly closed.
For use in the stable and outside.

Very rare: both models.

No. 1 Tubular Lantern
1870 – 1884.

No. 1 burner, 5/8" wick.
Clear, ruby, green, and blue globes.
Hot blast.
Finish: bright tin.

After 1875 the spring lifter was no longer used and side tubes no longer had corner braces. This model is easily distinguished from the No. O by the two miniature crosses stamped into the bail clamp, to indicate that it had a No. 1 burner with a 5/8" wick.
For use in the stable and outside.

Very rare.

No. 1 Fine Brass Tubular Lantern
1870 – 1875.

No. O burner, 5/8" wick.
Hot blast.
Finish: brass.

Advertised as a highly polished lantern that would be attractive in the home or as a portable light.

Very rare.

In 1873, the New York *Daily Graphic* had a balloon constructed in which a Professor Wise was to fly from Brooklyn, New York, across the Atlantic. This Dietz lantern, silver-plated, was sent to the professor on the day he was to depart, accompanied by this poem:

> "Take this Lantern, Professor Wise,
> You may need it in the skies.
> Should you fall from your lofty height,
> Grasp this Lantern firm and tight;
> 'Twill light your way, without a doubt,
> While passing through your downward route;
> But may you reach your destination
> Amid the cheers of all creation,
> And with a hero's well-earned name,
> Return to your native shores again.
> The 'Graphic' then will be in glory;
> And one "Wise" man to tell the story
> Of the 'Graphic' Balloon's wondrous flight
> And the 'Dietz' Lantern's superior light."

The flight, however, was never made.

No. OO Tubular Lantern
1870 – 1874.

Height: 11".
Base size: 5 1/2" x 3 7/8".
Base height: 1 1/4".
No. O burner, 5/8" wick.
Hot blast.
Finish: tin, but may also have been offered in brass.

The 1874 model had a round bail (not shown).

Very rare.

No. 10 Brass Tubular Lantern
1881 – 1887.

Height: 10".
No. OO burner, 1/4" wick.
Cold blast.
Finish: brass.

A lady's lantern for inside the home, and, probably, to light the way to the outhouse. This was the first cold-blast lantern manufactured by Dietz, but no mention of its unusual design was made in the advertising.

Very rare.

United States Tin Tubular Lantern
1880 – 1887.

Height: 10".
No. O burner, 3/8" wick.
With or without globe guards.
Hot blast.
Finish: bright tin; also, the catalogs offered it in brass, although records show no production in brass, probably because the No. 10 Brass Tubular Lantern was being offered at the same time.

Very rare.

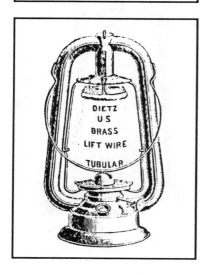

U.S. Brass and Nickel-Plate Tubular Lantern
1880 – 1905.

Height: 10 1/2".
No. O burner; 3/8" wick.
Hot blast.
Finish: From 1880 to 1887, bright tin or brass; by 1888, in brass or nickel-plate only.

1880 – 1887 models available with or without globe guards. By 1888, the bail came mounted to the side tubes, (as shown) instead of to a clamp on the top of the side tubes. For ladies to use around the home.

Rare.

No. O Best Lift Wire Lantern
1888 – 1905.

No. 1 burner, 5/8" wick.
Hot blast.
Finish: bright tin.

A No. O Tubular Lantern re-introduced, after eight years of no production, with a globe guard and other design changes. 1892 to 1905 models had support braces added from the font to the side tubes. General barn and outside use.

Rare: 1888 – 1891.

Very rare: 1892 – 1905.

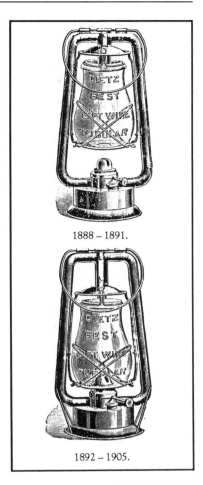

1888 – 1891.

Square Lift Lantern
1888 – 1904.

No. 1 burner, 5/8" wick.
Hot blast.

Made of tin, electroplated inside and out, it was highly polished, and is easily mistaken for copper or brass.

Rare.

1892 – 1905.

Best Square-Lift Lantern
1888 – 1904.

Hot blast.

Finished the same as the Square-Lift but with braces from the side tubes to the font for extra strength.

Very rare.

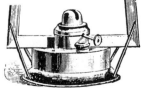

Best Square Lift Lantern.

Square Lift Lantern.

No. O Square Lift Tubular Lantern
1888 – 1904.

Hot blast.
*Finish: heavy brass, polished to a fine shine;
also available in nickel-plate.*

The font is dome shaped to add strength
to the side tubes.

Rare.

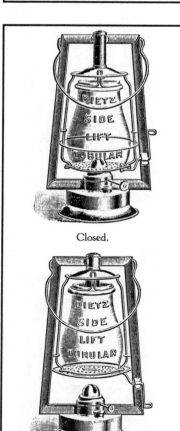

Closed.

Open.

No. 1 Side Lift Tubular Lantern
1890 – 1938.

Height: 13 1/2".
No. 1 burner, 5/8" wick.
Hot blast.
Finish: bright tin.

After 1938 sold overseas only, where it
found a good market.

Rare.

No. 2 Side Lift Tubular Lantern,
(not shown)
1892 – 1905

No. 2 burner, 1" wick.
Hot blast.

Similar style to No. 1.

Rare.

No. O Regular Tubular Lantern
1892 – 1902.

No. 1 burner, 5/8" wick.
Hot blast.
Finish: bright tin.

From 1903 to 1915 this was called the
No. O "Crown". These were simple,
inexpensive lanterns made for export
and sold extensively overseas.

Rare: 1892 – 1902.

Common: 1903 – 1915.

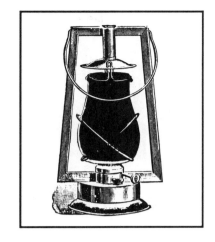

No. 2 Royal Tubular Lantern
1898 – 1915.

Height: 13 1/2".
No. 2 burner, 1" wick, 5 candlepower.
Hot blast.
Finish: bright tin.

In 1910 and later models, the crank was
moved from outside to inside the side
tube.

Rare: 1898 – 1909.

Common: 1910 – 1915.

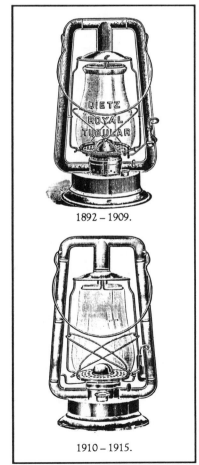

1892 – 1909.

1910 – 1915.

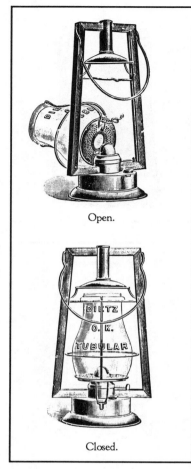

Open.

Closed.

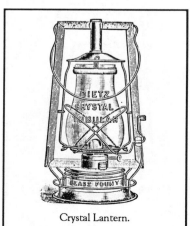

Crystal Lantern.

O.K. Lantern
1892 – 1915.

Height: 13".
No. 1 burner, 5/8" wick, 4 candlepower.
Hot Blast.
Finish: bright tin.

This is a square side-tube version of the Simplex Lantern (see p. 59).

Rare.

Crystal Lantern
1905 – 1920.

Height: 14".
No. 1 burner, 5/8" wick.
The font was of glass and replaceable.
Hot blast.
Finish: bright tin.
1905 – 1913 models had no globe
crank arm.

Designed for the construction trade, where it was a common practice to bury fonts in sand to hold lanterns steady. This hastened rust and corrosion, and the glass font was meant to minimize this or provide a quick replacement for a rotting font. (Later, double galvanizing was used to combat this problem.) The glass font also enabled the user to tell at a glance how much oil was left.
However, these easily breakable fonts did not sell well, so production was limited.

Rare: 1913 – 1920.

Very rare: 1905 – 1913.

Antifriction Tubular Lantern
1888 – 1903.

No. 1 burner, 5/8" wick.
This model had an unusual globe raiser.
Hot blast.
Finish: bright tin.

Very few of these were made, so it apparently did not attract buyers.

Very rare.

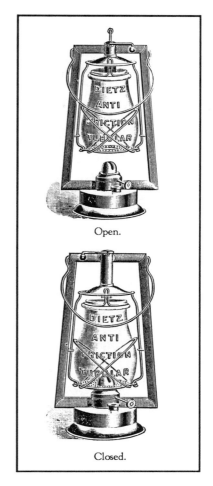

Open.

Closed.

Victor Lantern
1910 – 1939.

Height: 13 1/2".
No. 1 burner, 5/8" wick, 4 candlepower.
Hot blast.
Finish: bright tin, brass, and nickel-plate;
after 1915, bright tin only.
Domed font.

For household use (the finish was attractive for home use). After 1939 sold overseas only.

Rare.

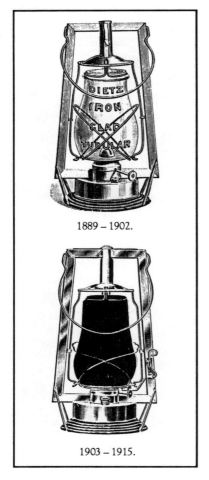

1889 – 1902.

1903 – 1915.

Iron Clad Lantern
1889 – 1915.

Height: 13 1/2".
No. 1 burner, 5/8" wick, 4 candlepower.
After 1902 a globe crank was added
(shown).
Hot blast.
Finish: bright tin, with heavy japanned font.

Designed for the construction trade, with a strongly supported font. The 1903 – 1915 version is shown with a colored globe, probably for highway department use.

Rare: both models.

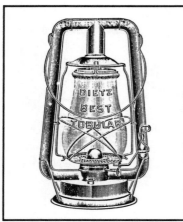

Best Tubular Lantern
1905 – 1912.

Hot blast.

Similar to the 1905 – 1912 Monarch Tubular Lantern (see p. 69), but with supports from the font to the side tubes, to make it stronger.

Designed for contractor use.

Rare.

Monarch Tubular Lantern
1905 – 1950

Height: 13 5/8".
No. 1 burner, 5/8" wick, 4 candlepower.
Hot blast.

A large font version of the No. O
Tubular Lantern (see p. 60), with globe
lifter on the outside of the side tubes.
The rare 1905 – 1912 style is shown.

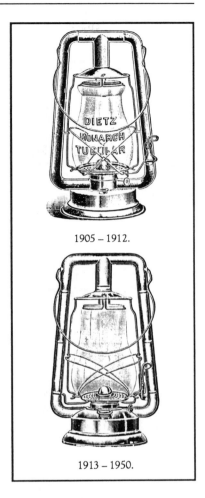

1905 – 1912.

The 1913 – 1950 style had a domed font
and the globe crank was moved inside
the side tubes. During 1914 to 1918 its
globe guards were styled differently
(shown).

Hot blast.
Finish: for all styles, bright tin.

Rare: 1905 – 1912 and the
1914 – 1918 variation.

Common: all other styles.

1913 – 1950.

Monarch Streamline Model
1938 – the 1960s.

Same specifications as the 1912– 1950
model, but "streamline" style and painted
blue.
Hot blast.

Very common.

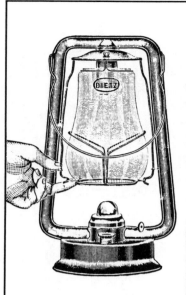

1899 – 1919.

Hy-Lo Lantern
1899 – 1945.

Height: 13 5/8"
No. 1 burner, 5/8" wick, 4 candlepower.
Note the three styles of globe guards with simple globe lift.
Hot blast.
Finish: bright tin.

Low-cost, general-purpose lantern.

Common: 1899 – 1919 and 1940 – 1945 models.

Very common: 1920 – 1939.

1940 – 1945.

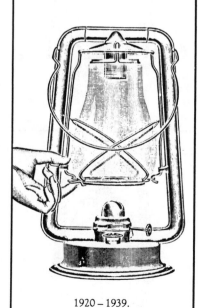

1920 – 1939.

Street Lantern
1873 – 1879.

Glass sides, 14" square formed
four separate doors.
No. 2 burner, 1" wick.
Glass font; internal chimney.
Dead flame.

Could be wall or post mounted. Also available for gas light fittings.

Very rare.

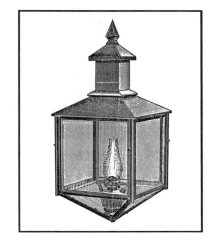

New York Street Lamp
1880 – 1887.

No. 2 burner, 1" wick.
Burned kerosene.
Internal chimney.
Dead flame.

Almost identical to 1873 Street Lantern (above) but with a burner style change and with the post socket as an integral part. The style shown was used in many districts of New York City.

Very rare.

Corporation Street Lamp
1879 – 1900.

No. 2 burner, 1" wick.
Burned kerosene.
Glass font; internal chimney.
Dead flame.

The removable cast-iron socket fit a post or bracket.
Gas conversion kit was available.

Very rare.

Square Tubular Street Lamp
1879 – 1900.

No. 3 slip burner, 1 1/2" wick.
Burned kerosene.
The "slip" burner was designed to extinguish
the flame after a fixed time period; burned
for 24 hours, each fill.
No internal chimney
Dead flame.

Gas conversion kit was available.

Very rare.

New York Street Lamp
1887 – 1897.

Height: 27"
No. 2 sun burner, 1" wick.
With mounting socket.
Dead flame.

Top made of corrugated tin to act as an
improved reflector.

Very rare.

No. 2 Square Tubular Street Lamp
1890 – 1914.

Height: 43".
No. 3 burner, 1 1/2" wick, 3" flame,
16 candlepower.
Cold blast.
Finish: heavy tin, painted green.

Rare.

No. 3 Globe Tubular Street Lamp
1880 – 1887.

Height: 25 1/2".
No. 3 burner, 1 1/2" wick, 22 candlepower.
No. 3 globe.
Cold blast.
Finish: tin only, painted black.

Very rare.

No. 3 Globe Tubular Street Lamp
1888 – 1906.

Height: 25 1/2" (tin); 24 1/2" (brass).
Finish: tin or brass, painted black.

More of these two models were sold than all other streetlights together.

Rare.

Fount and Burner
For No. 3 Globe Street Lamp.

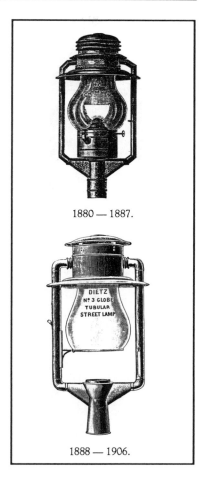

1880 — 1887.

1888 — 1906.

Pioneer Street Lamp
1906 – 1944.

Similar to No. 3 Globe Tubular Street Lamp but with a different name.
Colored globes available: red (fire station); blue (police station); green (hospital).
Brass or glass font.
Finish: tin or brass, painted green.

For years these No. 3's were the standard lamp for the U.S. government – used, for example, on Army and Navy bases.

Common.

1880 — 1887.

1888 — 1914.

No. 3 Globe Tubular Hanging Lamp
1880 –1887.

Height: 22".
No. 3 burner, 1 1/2" wick, 22 candlepower.
No. 3 globe.
Cold blast.
Finish: heavy tin, painted green.

Wire (skeleton) or solid base;
glass or brass font.

Very rare.

No. 3 Globe Tubular Hanging Lamp
1888 –1914.
Slight style changes but similar
specifications to 1880 – 1887 model.

If ordered with reflector attached, it was
called a **Side Tubular Lantern.**

Rare.

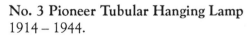

Reflector Attachment.

No. 3 Pioneer Tubular Hanging Lamp
1914 – 1944.

Slight style changes but similar
specifications to 1888 – 1914 model.
Also available with glass or brass font
as a special order.

Common.

No. 2 Globe Tubular Side and Globe Tubular Hanging Lamps
1888 – 1912.

No. 2 burner, 1" wick.
No. 2 Globe Side Lamp reflector was removable.
Cold blast.
Finish: heavy tin, painted green.

After 1910, orders for this lantern were filled with the No. 3 Globe Tubular Hanging Lamp. (See p. 74).

Rare.

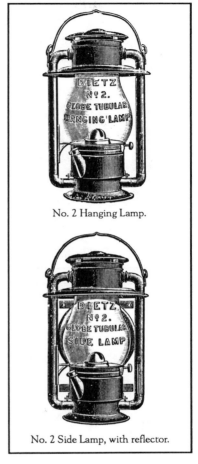

No. 2 Hanging Lamp.

No. 2 Side Lamp, with reflector.

No. 2 Climax Tubular Car Lamp
1892 – 1910.

No. 2 burner, 1" wick.
No. 2 globe; corrugated nickel-plate reflector.
Cold blast.
Finish: polished brass.

Very rare.

1888 – 1892.
Heavier model, with square joints at cross-pieces for better support (not shown).

Very rare.

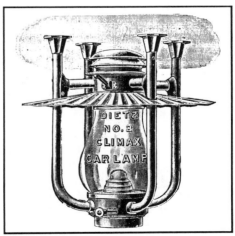

The lanterns on these next two pages had a unique way of supplying air to the flame by drawing it down through the handle. This reduced flickering when the lanterns were carried. They were for indoor use only. All burned sperm oil.

No. 1 Tubular Hand Lantern
1880 – 1897.

No. 1 burner; 5/8" wick.
Dead flame.
Finish: bright tin.

Very rare.

Bestov Hand Lamp
1898 –1920.

Height: 10"; 6 candlepower.
Dead flame.
Finish: bright tin.

This was an improved, No. 1 Tubular Hand lantern. Each was packed with a bracket to mount it on the wall.

Rare.

No. 11 Tubular Hand or Side Lantern
1892 – 1905.

No. 1 hinged Sun burner with underskirt (to hold chimney in place); 5/8" wick.
Corrugated metal reflector.
Dead flame.

Advertised as a safe, strong hand lantern that would not blow out with motion.

Very rare.

No. 2 Tubular Socket Lamp
1890 – 1897.

No. 2 hinged Sun burner, with under skirt;
1" wick.
5" silvered-glass reflector.
Dead flame.

Used as a side, hand, or table lantern.
Every lamp was packaged with a bracket
for wall mounting.

Very rare.

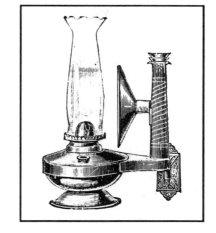

Bull's-Eye Police Lantern
1881 – 1887.

Two sizes: 7 1/4" high; 2 3/4" bull's-eye lens.
7 3/4" high; 3" bull's-eye lens.
Dead flame.
Finish: japanned black.
Made for police, but sold to the general
public as well.
Rare.

1888 – 1918.
Height: 8"; 3 candlepower.
Dead flame.
Finish: brown japanned.
Common.

Bull's-Eye Police Flash Lantern
1888 – 1918.

Height: 8"; 3 candlepower.
In 1894 the 2 3/4" lens was discontinued
on both models.
Dead flame.
Finish: brown japanned or all brass.

The flash lantern could be used to flash
(signal) for help.

Rare.

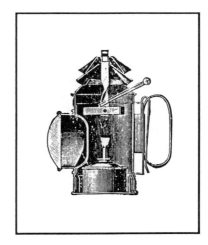

Closed with Pad Lock.

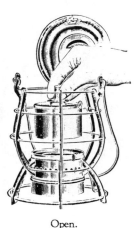

Open.

Mill Tubular Lantern
1902 – 1910.

No. 1 or No. 2 burner,
5/8" wick or 1" wick.
Hot blast.
Finish: bright tin.

Could be locked so that there was no access to the flame, for reasons related to insurance. Used by night watchmen as a safe lantern in high-fire-risk areas. The lantern was strong and heavily guarded and could be dropped with little danger of fire. Because it was locked, it could not be used to light a pipe or cigarette and possibly spill fuel while doing so. The lantern also had a "wind break guard" which helped to keep the lantern lit in windy locations.

Very rare.

Steel-clad Watchman's Safety Lantern
1903 – 1925.

Height: 10 1/4".
1903 – 1914, signal oil burner only.
1915 – 1925, available with a kerosene
burner, which came with a wick scraper to
remove char from the wick without opening
lantern. After 1917 it also was sold as the
Watchman's Mill Lantern.
Dead flame.
Finish: bright tin;
1918 and after, painted red.

A model with 100-hour, square font, painted red was available, with minimum order of 25 dozen for highway departments.

The oil font was inserted from the top, an assurance against its being lost. (Usually oil fonts were inserted from the bottom and might drop out.) This lantern, like the Mill Tubular, could be locked to satisfy insurance requirements.

Rare.

Underwriters Mill Lantern
1910 – 1946.

Height: 13 3/8".
No. 1 burner, 5/8" wick, 4 candlepower.
Hot blast.
Finish: bright tin; 1914 and after, painted red.

Approved by insurance companies, its globe could be padlocked to satisfy their requirements. Used in fire-risk areas.

Rare.

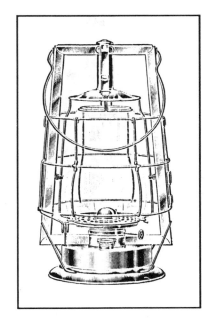

Night Watch Lantern
1945 – 1953.

Height: 8".
13/32" wick; 100-hour font.
Dead flame.
Finish: painted contractor yellow.

Fresnel lens. Named after a French physicist, this type of lens has a surface made up of many smaller lenses arranged in a manner that produces a short focal length. It typically was used in search-lights and spotlights, where great intensification of light was needed.

Sold as a highway contractor's lantern.

Very common: with red Fresnel lens.

Common: with clear Fresnel lens.

No. 1, No. 1 Burner.

No. 2, No. 2 Burner.

No. 1 and No. 2 Blizzard Mill Lantern
1910 – 1934.

Height: No. 1, 13 3/4".
No. 2, 14 3/4".
Burner: No. 1, 6 candlepower, No. 1 burner.
No. 2, 10 candlepower, No. 2 burner.
No. 1 and No. 2 used different globes.
Cold blast.
Finish: bright tin, 1910 – 1919;
painted red , 1920 – 1934.

Could be locked as safety measure.

Rare: both models.

No. 87 Weighted Bottom.

Torches
1950 – 1960.

Used by road contractors as highway markers, they are not lanterns.

Shown: No. 87, with a weighted bottom.

Net Capacity .... 3 Quarts
Diameter .... 8 Inches
Burns .... 30 Hours
Burner #87 .... Screw Type
Fuel. .... Kerosene
Wick .... 3/4 Inch Round
Body Height ..... 6 1/2 Inches
Finish .... Blue Enamel
(also special colors
to order)

Two-in-One Table Lantern
1910 – 1914.

Height: 13".
No. 1 burner, 5/8" wick, 6 candlepower,
burned for 13 hours.
Clear globes only.
Cold blast.
Finish: bright tin, brass or nickel-plate,
except, in 1913, available in tin only.
Designed with a nicer finish than usual
for outdoor lanterns, it was used indoors
as well.

Very rare.

Junior Lantern
1898 – 1946.

Height: 11 3/4".
No. 1 burner, 5/8" wick, 6 candlepower.
By 1914 was made with a different guard.
1898 – 1913 models had the globe-lifter
crank on the outside of the side tubes; in
later models it was on the inside.
Cold blast.
Finish: bright tin, or brass, or nickel-plate.

Some 1914 – 1918 models were stamped
with Hindi writing. These were an
Indian contract overrun. (See p. 30.)

Common.

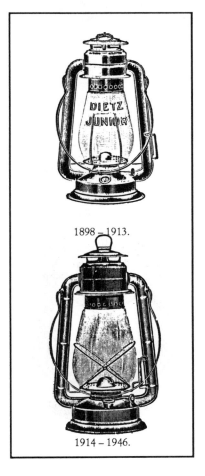

1898 – 1913.

1914 – 1946.

Junior Lantern
1939 – 1960s

Height: 12".
5/8" wick, 6 candlepower.
Cold blast.
Finish: painted iridescent blue.
Similar to the 1898 – 1946 Junior Lantern,
but streamlined models.

Advertised as selling well to Boy Scout
units for camping.

Very common.

Junior Lantern (not shown)
1989.

A copy of the 1898 –1946 model, issued to
commemorate Dietz's 150th anniversary.
Finish: all brass or painted red or blue.

Easy to distinguish from older models as
no patent dates are stamped onto this
lantern.

Comet Lantern
1939 – 1960s.

Height: 8 1/2".
13/32" wick, 4 candlepower.
Clear and ruby globes available.
Cold blast.
Finish: painted red or blue.

In 1953 this lantern was packaged with a
16-oz. can of Dietz odorless lantern fuel.
This offer apparently was not successful,
as it was discontinued. It would be rare
to find one of these packages. From
1939 to 1945 these lanterns were sold
overseas only; after 1945 they were sold
in the United States as well.
Officially approved by the Boy Scouts of
America for camping.

Very common.

Little Wizard Lantern

1920 – 1960s (to the 1980s from Dietz Hong Kong factory).

Height: 11 1/2".
5/8" wick, 6 candlepower.
Cold blast.

Available with a square, 100-hour font, painted red for highway contractors, in minimum orders of 25 dozen only. From 1925 on, it was available for police as a special order with green globes for traffic control. Also made as a patio or post light with an amber globe and a post socket underneath.

Very common.

Rare: as a patio light.

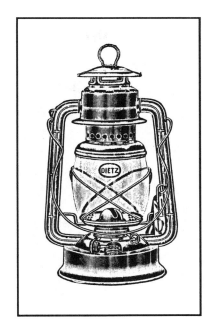

Little Wizard Streamline Lantern

1938 – 1980s.

Similar in size to the Little Wizard, but streamlined and painted blue. After the 1960s, manufactured only in Hong Kong. Cold blast.

Very common.

Original Dietz - 76 Lantern (not shown)

1976.

Font marked "Original Dietz - 76," top marked "Made In Hong Kong."
Finish: painted black with brass bail, globe guard and burner assembly.

Very similar to the Little Wizard but only 10" high. Sold for one year only in the United States to celebrate the bicentennial, hence the "76" on the font.

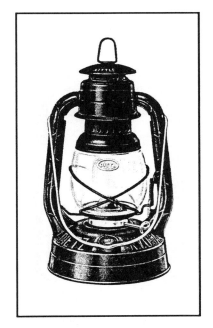

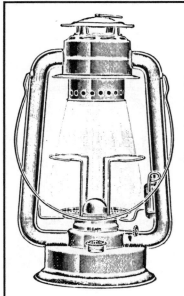

1912 – 1919.

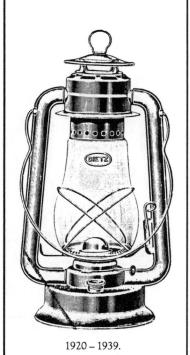

1920 – 1939.

No. 2 Crescent Lantern
1912 – 1939.

Height: 15".
Burner No. 262, 1" wick, 10 candlepower.
Clear, ruby, blue, and green globes.
Cold blast.
From 1912 to 1920, made with an unusual globe guard not found on any other Dietz lanterns before or after.
Finish: tin, except, in last year of manufacture, (1939) painted red only.

After 1939, sold overseas only.

Rare: 1912 – 1919.

Common: 1920 – 1939.

No. 2 Crescent Lantern
1939 – 1960s.

Cold blast.
Finish: bright tin (for overseas only); painted red in U.S.A. up to 1945, thereafter painted blue.

Similar to
1912 – 1939
Crescent
Lantern, but
streamlined
model.

Very common.

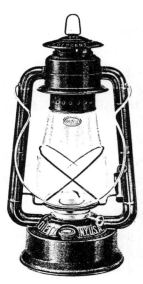

1939 – 1960s.

Little Star Lantern
1912 – 1939.

Height: 11".
No. 1 burner, 5/8" wick, 3 candlepower.
Hot blast.
Finish: bright tin, except from 1930 to 1939, painted red.

Rare.

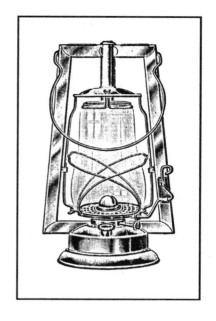

Little Giant Lantern
1939 – 1960s.

Height: 11 1/2".
5/8" wick, 6 candlepower; 70-hour font.
Also available with a 100-hour font as a special order.
Cold blast.

This was a streamlined version of Little Star Lantern, advertised as "fully automated."

A contractor's lantern.

Common.

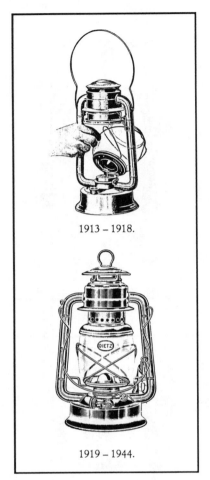

1913 – 1918.

1919 – 1944.

D-Lite Lantern
1913 – 1944.

Height: 13 1/4".
No. 2 burner, 1" wick, 10 candlepower.
The 1913– 1918 style had a top dome
crank; after 1918, the crank was moved to
the more standard location on the side tube.
Red, blue, and green globes available.
Cold blast.
Finish: 1913 – 1918: bright tin; bright tin
with a brass font; bright tin with brass font
and dome. After 1918, bright tin only,
except that in late 1939 an unsuccessful
attempt was made to re-introduce a
brass font.

The D-Lite was a very good seller,
designed by Warren McArthur, Jr., who
in 1912 was a sales agent for Dietz and
for the C. T. Ham Company. He called
this the "Short Globe" lantern, but it was
sold as the "D-Lite."

Rare: 1913 – 1918.

Common: 1919 – 1944.

D-Lite Lantern
1939 – 1960s.

Similar to the 1919 – 1944 D-Lite,
but streamlined model.
Cold blast.
Finish: painted iridescent blue,
1940 – 1960s; in 1939, painted red only.

Very common.

No. 2 Tubular Square Beach Lamp
1888 – 1912.

No. 3 burner, 1 1/2" wick.
Side wings and back fitted with corrugated silvered-glass reflector.
Made with a socket to fit on a post; socket mount sold as an option.
Cold blast.

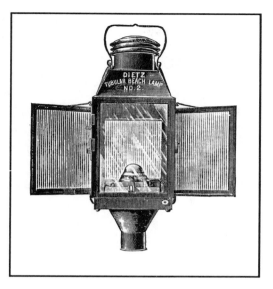

This expensive and attractive lamp was not advertised, but parts were manufactured for it through 1910. No other information was available for it prior to 1888, but it may be the "No. 2 Bow Lamp," for boats, mentioned in some 1885 parts lists. The presumption is that it was for government sale only, perhaps for use by the Coast Guard. After 1898, its name was changed and it was sold as the **No. 2 Beach Lamp.**

Very rare.

No. 2 Tubular Square Guarded Government Lantern
1888 – 1906.

Height: 22 1/2"
No. 2 burner, 1" wick.
Corrugated silvered-glass reflector; colored sheet glass panels available.
Hot blast.
Finish: tin, painted black.

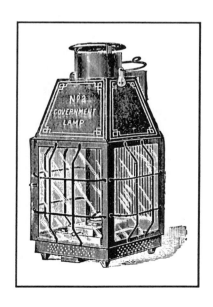

Used extensively by the U.S. government; too expensive for broad sale to the general public.

Very rare.

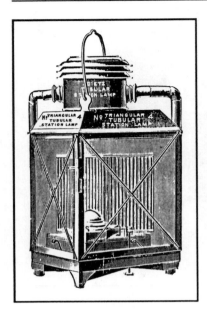

No. 4 Tubular Triangular Lantern
1888 – 1905.

Height: 22"; width: 16"; depth: 13".
No. 3 burner, 1 1/2" wick.
Cold blast.
Finish: tin, painted black.

This triangular lamp fitted easily into
a corner.

*"No Chimney. Improved Burner. Does not
smoke. Light output equal to gas at a lower cost.
Flame regulated from the outside. Will not blow
out in the strongest wind. Reflector arranged to
throw light in three different directions."*

Very rare.

No. 2 and No. 3 Triangular
Station Lanterns
1890 – 1905.

No. 2.
Weight: 8 1/2 lbs.
No. 2 burner, l" wick.
8" silvered-glass reflector.
Dead flame.
Finish: bright tin, painted black.

Very rare.

No. 3.
Weight: 13 lbs.
No. 2 burner, 1" wick.
10" silvered-glass reflector.
Dead flame.
Finish: bright tin, painted black.

The No. 2 and the No. 3 were identical
in style, with the No. 2 being slightly
smaller.

Note the burner with internal chimney.
This inner lantern could be removed and
carried as a portable light.

Very rare.

Nos. 1, 2, and 3 Tubular Square Lantern
1880 – 1887.

No. 1.
Height: 14"; width: 8"; depth: 8".
No. 1 burner, 5/8" wick.
6" silvered-glass reflector.

No. 2.
Height: 18"; width: 10"; depth: 10 ".
No. 2 burner, 1" wick.
7" silvered-glass reflector.

No. 3
Height: 20"; width: 12 1/2"; depth: 12 1/2".
No. 3 burner, 1 1/2" wick.
12" silvered-glass reflector.
Hot blast.

Designed for use in mills, mines, shops, and barns.

Very rare.

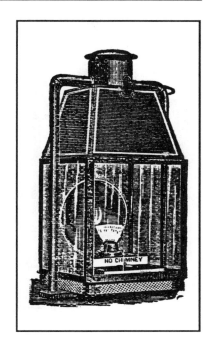

Nos. 1, 2, and 3 Tubular Square Lantern
1888 – 1894.

No. 1.
Height: 19"; width: 8 1/2"; depth: 9".
1" wick, 6" silvered-glass reflector.

No. 2.
Height: 21 1/2"; width: 9 5/8"; depth: 10 1/2".
1 1/2" wick, 8" silvered-glass reflector.

No. 3.
Height: 26"; width: 13 3/4"; depth: 13".
1 1/2" wick, 12" silvered-glass reflector.
Cold blast.

No. 1, No. 2, and No. 3 were identical in style, No. 3 being the largest. From 1894 to 1914, all three were sold as the **Improved Tubular Square Lantern,** finished in japanned blue. In 1914, the No. 1 and No. 3 styles were discontinued. The No. 2 was sold until 1924 as the **Imperial Square Lantern.**

Very rare.

Climax Station Lamp

No. 1: 1913 – 1920.
No. 2: 1913 – 1945.
No. 3: 1913 – 1920.

See original catalog specifications below.
Dead flame.
Finish: japanned blue.

No. 3 remained in the catalogs up to 1920 but was not actually available after 1916.

Rare: No. 1.

Common: No. 2.

Very rare: No. 3.

Note the chimney-size numbers. By the 20th century, various manufacturers had begun to standardize sizes among themselves. The chimney shown here reveals a modern design: the frilly top is more decorative than that of earlier chimneys.

	Size No. 1	Size No. 2	Size No. 3
Height Over All	15"	17 1/2"	20"
Extreme Width	8 3/4"	10 1/4"	11 1/2"
Extreme Depth	7 1/8"	8 3/4"	10 1/2"
Reflected Light by Test	—	—	—
Size of Wick	5/8"	1"	1"
Burner	No. 1 chimney	No. 2 chimney	No. 2 chimney
Size of Silvered Glass Reflector	7"	8"	10"

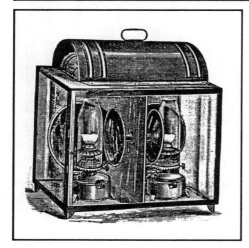

Double Bow Top Station Lamp
1878 – 1885.

This 14" x 19" lamp was fitted with two 7" and two 8" reflectors and two No. 2 burners. It reflected light in three directions.
Dead flame.
Finish: tin, painted black.

The lamps on this page are examples of internal chimneys (or globes) within a glass framework (see p. 23).

Very rare.

Square Station Lamps

No. 1.

1880 – 1887.

8" x 12".
5/8" wick, burned
kerosene.
7" silvered-glass reflector.

No. 2.

1880 – 1914.

10" x 14".
1" wick, burned kerosene.
8" silvered-glass reflector.

No. 3.

12" x 16".
1" wick.
10" silvered-glass reflector.
All are dead flame.
Finish: painted black.

Very rare: as a set.

Rare: singly.

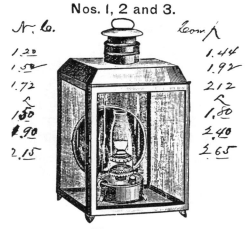

Square Station Lamps,

Nos. 1, 2 and 3.

Three Sizes.

FOR KEROSENE.

No. 1 is 8x12 inches, with ⅝-inch wick and 7-inch
Silvered Glass Reflector.
No. 2 is 10x14 inches, with 1-inch wick and 8-inch
Silvered Glass Reflector..
No. 3 is 12x16 inches, with 1-inch wick and 10-inch
Silvered Glass Reflector.

The above three sizes nest in packing.

PACKED IN NESTS OF THREE EACH.

Note the handwriting above. A nineteenth century sales-
man was figuring wholesale and retail prices, at 20 percent

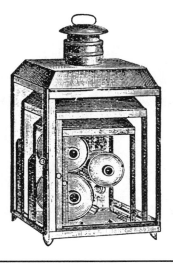

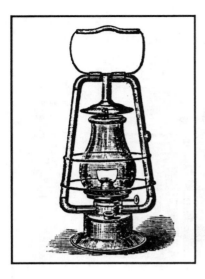

New York Fire Department Tubular Lantern
1881 – 1887.

No. 1 burner, 5/8" wick.
Hot blast.
Finish: bright tin.

These were made of special heavy steel, tin plated, and very strong, for fire companies. Only a few were made completely of brass.

Very rare.

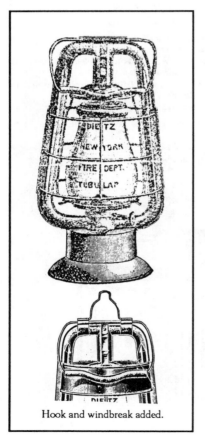

Hook and windbreak added.

Tubular Fire Department Lantern
1888 – 1912.

No. 1 burner, 5/8" wick.
Hot blast.
Finish: all brass; nickel-plate; bright tin, with copper font.

In 1904 an extra hook was added to this model for fastening the lantern on fire truck lantern hangers. A windbreak also was added.

Fire department lanterns were constantly exposed to water, so brass and copper were valued fire lantern materials, because they did not rust.

Rare.

King Fire Lantern
1907 – 1940.

Height: 14".
No. 1 burner, 5/8" wick, 4 candlepower.
Hot blast.
Finish: polished brass; nickel-plated brass;
bright tin with copper font (not available
after 1913); bright tin; silver-plated brass.

Different-color bull's-eye lenses, fastened
to the globe plate, identified officers'
lanterns, so officers could be easily
located at a fire scene. Half-colored
globes were available: upper part green,
ruby, or blue; lower part clear. All these,
and globes engraved with the fire
company name, could be special ordered.

An August 1939 memo stopped production of King Fire Lanterns because of
slow sales. In January 1940, instructions
were issued to paint remaining stocks
red, to slow corrosion, and to close out
stock by selling to fire and construction
companies.

Rare.

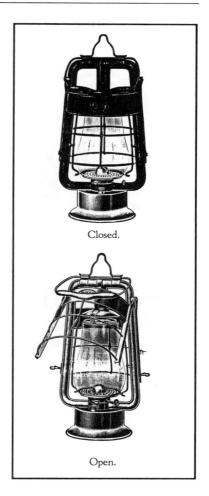

Closed.

Open.

Queen Brass Fire Tubular Lantern
1901 – 1910.

No. 1 burner, 5/8" wick.
Hot blast.
Finish: polished brass; nickel-plate.

Bull's- eye lens was available, mounted
on the globe plate in one of the
following colors, designating differing
officer ranks: white, red, blue, amber,
or green.

Very rare.

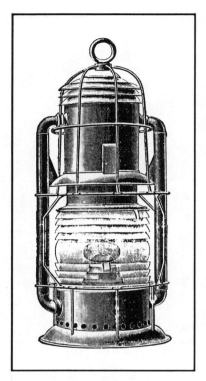

Improved No. 1 and No. 2 Tubular Marine Signal Lamp
1888 – 1912.

Height: very large lanterns,
approximately 30" high.
No. 1: No. 1 burner, 5/8" wick.
No. 2: No. 2 burner, 1" wick.
With an optional Fresnel lens or globe the light
could be seen at greater distances.
Different-color Fresnel globes were available.
Cold blast.
Finish: tin or brass.

Used by the Signal Service and Light House Departments of the U.S.A. and Canada.

The word "improved" signals that this is not the first of its type made, but there are no records of a previous model by Dietz, of this lantern. It may be that prior to 1888 Dietz sold, under its own name, marine lamps made by Dennis & Wheeler. When the latter went out of business, in 1881, and was absorbed by the Steam Gauge and Lantern Company, Dietz probably continued to buy from them. In 1888 Dietz began to make their own Tubular Marine Signal Lamps.

Very rare: both models.

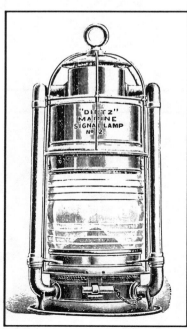

No. 1 and No. 2 Hinged Tubular Marine Signal Lamps
1888 – 1912.

No. 1: No. 1 burner, 5/8" wick.
No. 2: No. 2 burner, 1" wick.
Different-color Fresnel globes available.
Cold blast.
Finish: bright tin. Probably available in brass as
well, but no records were found to confirm this
assumption.

For use on buoys in harbors and difficult-to-navigate waterways.

Very rare: both models.

No. 39 Standard Railroad Lantern
1888 – 1912.

Burned lard oil, signal oil, or kerosene,
using different burners for each.
Glass oil font available as an extra as well as
double and single guards.
Dead flame.
Finish: brass or nickel-plate in single-guard
lantern. Double guard, bright tin only.

Common: tin.

Rare: brass or nickel-plate.

No. 39 Improved Standard Railroad Lantern
1912 – 1946.

Height: 10".
2 candlepower.
Shown with dark-colored globe.
Dead flame.
Finish: bright tin.

Very common.

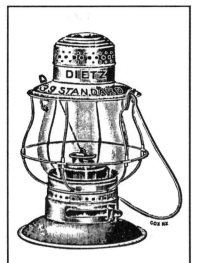

Single guard.

Double guard.

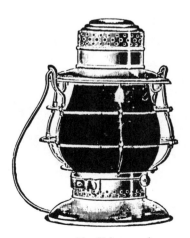

No. 39 Improved

No. 43 Railroad Lantern
1888 – 1905.

Burned lard oil only and had a Sangster spring oil pot.
Dead flame.
Finish: tin, brass, or nickel-plate.

Rare: tin.

Very rare: brass or nickel-plate.

No. 43 1/2 (not shown)

Was a double-guard version of this lantern.

Midwestern railroads used cheap, locally available lantern fuel–typically, animal fats (lard)–not whale oil. This fat congealed in cold temperatures, so the lanterns using these fuels were not very efficient.

Rare.

Single guard.

No. 39 Vulcan Railroad Lantern
1888 – 1912.

Burned lard oil or signal oil.
Available with single or double guard and inside or outside wick adjuster.
Dead flame.
Finish: bright tin.

Rare: both styles.

Double guard.

Improved Vulcan Railroad Lantern
1912 – 1946.

Height: 10".
1" wick, 2 candlepower.
Dead flame.
Finish: bright tin.

Very common.

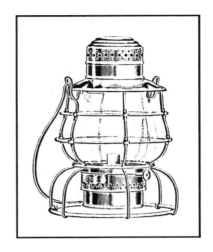

No. 39 Steel Clad Railroad Lantern
1888 – 1910.

Burned signal oil or kerosene.
Available with single or double guard and
outside or inside wick adjuster, all with
two-piece guard supports.
Dead flame.
Finish: bright tin.

Common: all styles.

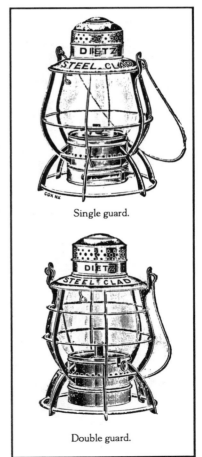

Single guard.

Double guard.

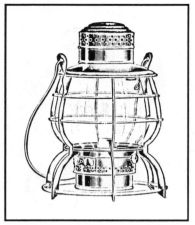

Improved Steel Clad Railroad Lantern
1910 – 1950.

Height: 10".
1" wick, 2 candlepower.
Dead flame.
Finish: bright tin.
Guard supports in this model were one-piece
of stamped steel .

Very common.

Improved Steel Clad Lantern (not shown)
1940 – 1950.

Large font, with top marked "8 Day Burning."

Sold to highway contractors.

Steelclad Lantern
1950 – 1960s.

Height: 10".
No. 391 burner. 5/8" wick, 1 candlepower.
(This unusual burner is still being used today on
railroads in Third World countries.)

This is similar to the 1888 – 1910 No. 39
Steel Clad Railroad Lantern, with slight
changes, and introduced under a new name.

Very common.

No. 7 Gem Oil Lantern
1871 – 1880.

Burned sperm oil. Refer to p. 17 for details
of two-tube burner.
Dead flame.

"It has a two-tube Oil Burner, removable
Globe, Glass Oil Fount that can be detached
from the bottom in a moment, and a corrugated
band at the top. It makes a first-class Railroad
Oil Lantern.

No. 8 is the same as above, fitted with
Kerosene Burner."

Very rare.

No. 9 Champion Railroad or Ship Lantern
1870 – 1885.

Dead flame.

By 1881 called simply No. 9 Champion.

Very rare.

"The Champion Railroad or Ship Lantern is larger than the Vesta, and has a larger glass and stronger frame, also a corrugated band at the top. The glass and oil pot are removable. The glass can be detached from the frame, cleansed and replaced in a moment. It is one of the best and strongest Lanterns for ship or railroad use. Also the same in brass."

New Vesta Railroad Lantern
1906 – 1912.

Cold blast.
Finish: bright tin.

Rare.

New Vesta Railroad Lantern
1913 – 1920.

Height: 11"; 3 candlepower.
Cold blast.
Finish: bright tin or all brass.

Common: tin.

Rare: brass.

1906 – 1912.

1913 – 1920.

Vesta Lantern
1920 – 1950s.

Cold blast.
Finish: bright tin or all brass.

This model's base support was changed to a design stronger than that of the 1912 – 1920 Vesta lantern, and after 1940 its oil font was crimped to add strength as well. Rigid fiber bails on this model were specially ordered for electric rail use, as they were nonconductive. They could be locked into a rigid, upright position.

Very common: tin.

Rare: brass.

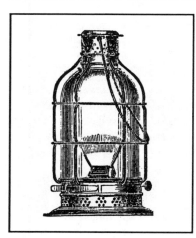

No. 6 Vesta
1870 – 1880.

"B" burner (precursor of the No. 2),
1" wick, outside wick adjuster.
Dead flame.
Finish: tin or brass.

84,000 sold in 1873.

Very rare.

No. 6 Vesta
1880 – 1887.

No. 2 burner, 1" wick, burned kerosene.
Dead flame.
Finish: tin.

The earlier No. 6 Vesta was a popular model, but the factory fire of 1880 probably destroyed the dies and equipment, forcing a major redesign.

Very rare.

No.. 39 Conductor's Lantern and No. 39 Fireman's Lantern
1888 – 1905.

Burns lard oil or signal oil.
Dead flame.
Finish: brass or nickel-plate.

Exactly the same lantern except for the loop, which was common on the firemen's lamps. ("Fireman" here refers to the fireman on the railroad.)

Common: No. 39 Conductor's Lantern.

Very rare: No. 39 Fireman's Lantern.

No. 3 Conductor's Lantern
1888 – 1920.

Height: 9 1/2"; 1 candlepower.
Burned lard oil or signal oil.
Dead flame.
Finish: Brass or nickel-plate; also, gold or silver plated to order.

Rare.: brass or nickel-plate.

Very rare: gold or silver plated.

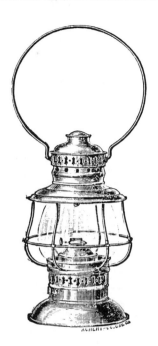

No. 39 Conductor's Lantern.

No. 3 Conductor's Lantern.

No. 39 Fireman's Lantern.

No. 8 Conductor's Lantern
1888 – 1920.

Same specifications as No. 3, except had skeleton base added over font.

The No. 3, 8, and 39 lanterns can, rarely, be found with half color globes and engraved with the owner's name. Lanterns with such etching are examples of the kind of special feature that makes specific lanterns command higher prices than usual.

No. 74 Lantern (not shown)
1871 – 1913.

Dead flame.

Similar to the A No. 1 lantern (see p. 105) but marked No. 74.

Very rare.

1882 – 1891.

No. 74 Lantern
1882 – 1891.

No. 1 Convex burner, 5/8" wick.
Candle socket supplied with lantern could be interchanged with the kerosene burner.
Ruby, green, or white globe available.
Dead flame.
Finish: bright tin.

Very rare.

1892 – 1913.

No. 74 Lantern
1892 – 1913.

Height: 10 3/4".
Convex burner, 5/8" wick, but unlike the other No. 74 convex burner designs.
Different globe and oil pot (font) from the two preceding models.
Available with clear globe only.
Finish: bright tin.

Rare.

A No. 1 Lantern
1880 – 1896.

Height: 10 3/4".
Convex burner, (see p. 19),
5/8" wick for kerosene.
Two round wick burner for sperm oil
(shown); candle adapter.
For oil, candle, or kerosene.
Ruby, green, and clear globes available.
Dead flame.
Finish: bright tin.

Very rare.

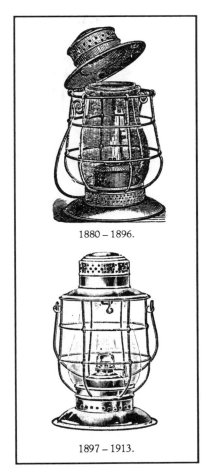

1880 – 1896.

A No. 1 Lantern
1897 – 1913.

Slightly different in style from the earlier
model, and the burner and other details
were modernized.

Rare.

1897 – 1913.

No. 14 Lantern
1870 – 1874.

Dead flame.

"No. 14 is a patent lantern for oil,
kerosene or candles." Probably came
with three burner attachments (see p.
52). The sales caption noting that the
lamp was patented implies its quality
(i.e., worth patenting).

Very rare.

"No. 14 is a patent Lantern for oil,
kerosene or candles."

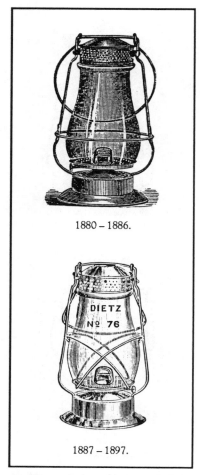

1880 – 1886.

1887 – 1897.

No. 76 Lantern
1880 – 1886.

No. 1 burner, 5/8" wick.
Clear and colored (shown) globes.
Dead flame.

Very rare.

No. 76 Lantern
1887 – 1897.

No. 1 burner, 5/8" wick.

The globe guard was changed to the crossover style.

Rare.

Diamond Brass Safety Lantern
1877 – 1887.

Height: 7 1/2".
No. 1 convex burner, 5/8" wick, burned kerosene.
Dead flame.

Very rare.

Racket Brass Lantern
1881 – 1910.

No. 1 convex burner, 5/8" wick, for kerosene, burned 18 hours.
Dead flame.

"It is similar in size to the Diamond Lantern, and takes the same globe and same size burner. It is very simple in construction. It lights and regulates from outside."

Rare.

Boy Brass Safety Lantern
1881 – 1906.

No. O convex burner, 3/8" wick, for kerosene.
Dead flame.

Used by servants to tend to outside jobs at night, and popular as a children's lantern because of its small size. With globe guards added, this model was called the **Sport Lantern** (not shown).

Rare:Boy Brass Lantern.

Common: Sport Lantern.

"It is similar in form to the Racket Lantern, but much smaller, being only six inches in height. Easy to handle; lighted and regulated from the outside."

Baby Brass Lantern
1881 – 1906.

Height: 4 1/2".
Firefly burner, burned kerosene.
Dead flame.

Smallest lantern made by Dietz. Designed as a long-lasting night-light, it burned for twelve hours. In the 1880s, some experimental models were manufactured that used this lantern with a holder and clamp as a bicycle light.

Rare.

Protector Trackwalker's Lantern
1913 – 1945.

Height: 15 1/2"; 4 candlepower.
Hot blast.
Finish: bright tin.

Common.

*"This valuable lamp is designed to protect the life and facilitate the work of the railroad trackwalker. It is furnished with a hood reflector which hides the light from being seen from the rear except a three inch fixed white semaphore lens. Hidden in the hood is a three inch ruby movable lens **which may be instantly thrown between the flame and the fixed white lens, forming a strong, red danger signal.**"*

Acme Inspector's Lantern
1900 – 1945.

Height: 15 1/2".
No. 1 high-cone burner, 5/8" wick, 7 candlepower.
5" silvered-glass reflector, 6" deep hood.
Hot blast.
Finish: tin, painted black.

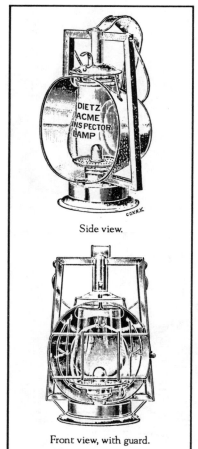

Side view.

Front view, with guard.

This lantern went through many design changes over the years. Most noticeably, in 1914 the curved handle was squared and supports were added from the side tubes to the font. A front guard was an option after 1915.

Used by the U.S. Life Saving Service as a patrol light, it also was very popular with railroad companies and police agencies. The hood focused the light well, and reduced back glare for the user.

Rare: 1900 – 1914.

Common: models after 1914.

Junior Inspector's Lantern
1914 – 1924.

Height: 11 1/4".
No. 1 burner, 5/8" wick, 6 candlepower.
Cold blast.
Finish: bright tin.
Also made with a handle similar to the
"Acme" Inspector's Lantern handle.

This lantern was suitable for ticket collectors and car checkers, because of its small size.

Very rare: without handle.

Rare: with handle.

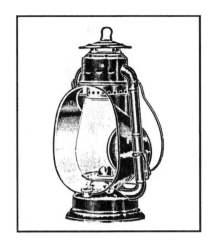

No. O Tubular Reflector Lantern
1875 – 1887.

No. 1 burner, 5/8" wick.
5" silvered-glass reflector inside a
nickel-plated hood.
In 1880 and later models, the spring lifter
was replaced with a straight-wire lifter.
Hot blast.
Finish: bright tin.

Very rare.

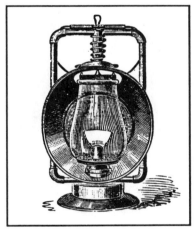

Vesta Rear Signal Lamp
1910 – 1925.

Height: 11"; 3 candlepower.
Cold blast.
Shown with colored globe.
Finish: bright tin.

Equipped with a bracket, it slid into a mounting on the trolley car.

Very rare.

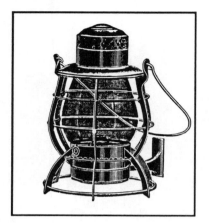

Rear Signal Lantern
1919 – 1925.

Height: 10".
Burned signal oil.
Shown with colored globe.
Dead flame.
Finish: redipped, bright tin.

Made for trolley cars as a rear light, with interchangeable colored globes to give different signals.

Rare.

X.L.C.R. Switchman's Lantern
1912 – 1916.

Height: 9".
Burned signal oil.
Bail had fiber-insulated grip for protection when working near "third rail" electric lines.
Dead flame.
Finish: redipped, bright tin.

Very rare.

Improved X.L.C.R. Switchman's Lantern
1914 – 1925.

Dead flame.
Finish: bright tin.

Burned signal oil. Equipped with a "wing lock" burner fitting into a slip collar and resting on a fiber washer permanently secured to the font. A short turn of the wrist securely locked the burner, making it spill-proof even if swung to signal. The small arrow points to the bail lock latch which could be raised to lock the bail into an upright position. Insulated bail for protection when working near "third rail" electric lines.

Rare.

No. 6 Railroad Lantern
(New York Central Pattern)
1901 – 1920.

Height: 10".
2 candlepower.
White, ruby, blue, and green globes available.
Dead flame.
Finish: bright tin.

Common.

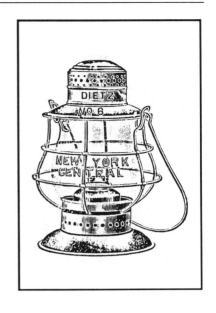

"Burns railroad signal oil. Can also be fitted with convex burner for kerosene.

This lantern is similar to the No. 39 Standard, the principal difference being that it has a Sangster spring oil pot instead of the bayonet catch.

Hinge top and removable globe.

Bail is attached to guard frame, and is so arranged that when the lantern is in use the bail stands upright. The bail can be thrown down on the base of the lantern if required.

The New York Central Railroad uses this lantern exclusively."

No. 999 Railroad Lantern
1950 – 1960.

Height: 8 7/8".
Dead flame.
Finish: flat, stamped steel, tinned.

For railroad signaling; sold in many other countries besides the United States. As an option, had the rigid, fiber bails special-ordered for electric-rail use.

Very common.

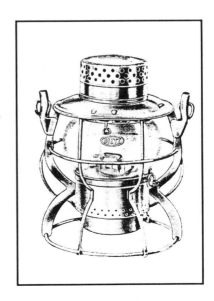

Navy Standard Deck Lantern
1914 – 1918.

Dead flame.

Similar to the 1912 – 1920 Vesta, but in brass and marked "Navy Standard." Used on ships of the United States Navy.

Very rare.

U. S. Lantern
1913 – 1920.

Height: 10".
5/8" wick, 2 candlepower.
Dead flame.
Finish: tin, painted red, yellow, blue or green.

Introduced to replace the Racket and Boy Lanterns.

Rare.

Carriage and Automobile Lamps

Some lanterns were hung under the body and to side of the vehicle (shown below), so that the light could be seen from back and front, to avoid being run into by another vehicle. Others were placed up on the dash board, or sides, to help light the way for the driver.

C. J. HAMLIN AND HIS CHAMPION TEAM, BELLE HAMLIN AND GLOBE.
Pole record over Elliptical Track, 2:13½, made at Belmont Park, Philadelphia, Pa., May, 1891.

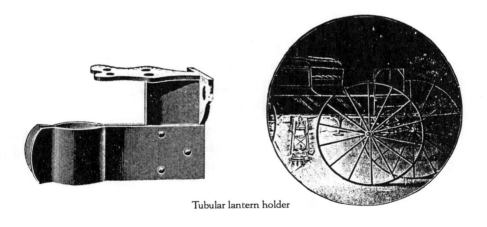

Tubular lantern holder

Junior Dash Lamp
1898 – 1910.

Height: 11 3/4".
No. 1 burner, 5/8" wick.
Cold blast.
Finish: painted black.

Globe crank on outside of side tubes.
Could be used as a wall, hand, or dash lamp.

Rare.

Junior Dash Lamp
1914 – 1920.

Height: 11 3/4".
No. 1 burner, 5/8" wick, 7 candlepower.
Cold blast.

Similar to 1898 – 1910 Junior Dash
Lamp but has a 2 1/4" bull's- eye lens
inside the globe, mounted on the globe
plate. Globe crank moved to inside of
tubes. May be found with or without
ruby round 2 1/4" lens mounted so light
could be seen from rear.

Common.

Junior Side, or Wagon Lamp
1914 – 1945.

Height: 11 3/4"; 7 candlepower.
Cold blast.

Similar to the Junior Dash Lamp, but
with side mounts and a 2 1/4" red
ruby rear lens so that light could be
seen from rear. A clear 2 1/4" bull's-
eye lens inside the globe mounted to
the globe plate.

Both post-1914 Junior Lamps commonly are found with Hindi writing
on them (see p. 30), indicating they
were part of an overrun of Junior
lanterns from an Indian contract.

Very common.

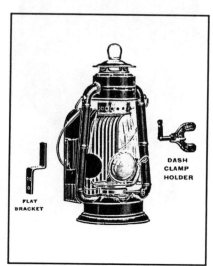

DASH
CLAMP
HOLDER

FLAT
BRACKET

Buckeye Dash Lamp
1898 – 1946.

Height: 13 1/2".
No. 1 burner, 5/8" wick, 10 candlepower.
Hot blast.
Finish: painted black.

Similar to No. 13 Tubular Side and Dash Lamp (see p. 116), but with a 2 1/4" bull's-eye lens and a globe lifter crank.

This lantern was also made in a larger size called a **Royal Dash Lamp** (not shown), which was 15" high, and had a No. 2 burner and 1" wick.

Very common.

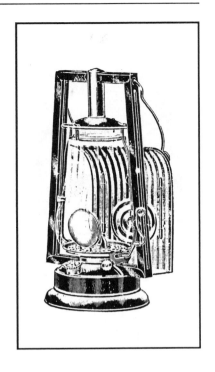

No. 1 Blizzard Dash Lamp
(not shown)
1898 – 1925.

No. 1 burner, 5/8" wick.
14 1/2-hour font.
Cold blast.
Finish: japanned blue.

Rare.

No. 2 Blizzard Dash Lamp
1898 – 1925.

Height: 14 1/2".
No. 2 burner, 1" wick, 10 candlepower.
19-hour font.
2 1/4" bull's-eye lens fused into globe, or mounted on globe plate (shown).
Cold blast.
Finish: painted black.
*Can also be found marked **"No. 1"** or*
__"No. 2 Cold Blast"__ and finished in
japanned blue.

Rare: all styles.

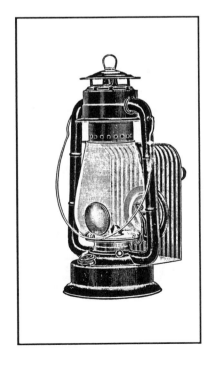

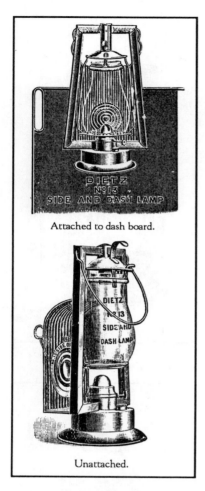

Attached to dash board.

Unattached.

No. 13 Tubular Side and Dash Lamp
1886 – 1897.

No. 1 burner, 5/8" wick.
No. O globe.
Hot blast.

A low-cost dash lantern.

Rare: all styles.

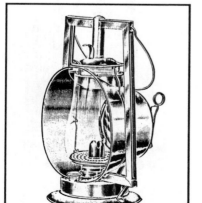

Beacon Dash Lamp
1905 – 1925.

Height: 14 1/2".
No. 1 long-cone burner, 5/8" wick,
7 candlepower.
No. O globe.
5" spun metal reflector.
Hot blast.

Similar to the No. O Reflector Tubular Lantern but re-introduced under another name, with side supports added between the font and side tubes.

Common.

No. O Tubular Reflector Lantern

1888 – 1905.

No. 1 long-cone burner, 5/8" wick.
No. O globe, 6" deep hood with 5" silvered-glass reflector.
Hot blast.

It had a rear bracket for attaching to auto dashboard.

Rare.

Dietz Union Driving Lamp

Attached to dash board.

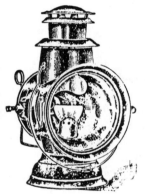

"All styles except the japanned (cheapest) are made with a flaring rim on the front door as above.

"Sectional cut showing circulation of air."

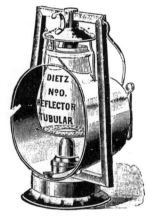

Unattached.

"A-holder."

"B-holder."

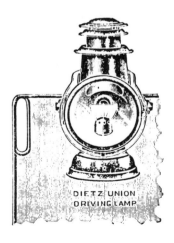

Cut showing Lens with Tin Rim.

This Dietz sales catalog copy reflects the changes from wagon to automobile headlights as cars became common.

Dietz Oil Lamps.

 e have been making lamps for 63 years and for the past 15 years have been making what we called our Tubular Driving Lamp, and selling them in large numbers all over the country, more especially to doctors for night driving. This was made on the well-known Tubular principle. The air was taken in under the projections on the top of the lamp, conducted to the burner through the hollow space between the reflector and the outside body of the lamp, supplying, in this way cold air to the burner. No air reached the burner except in this roundabout way. The result of this was that the wind blowing against the lamp did not effect the flame because of the course it had to pursue to reach the burner. This was also true of the shocks caused by bad roads. They did not effect the burning of the lamp materially. This lamp has met with the greatest success.

When the Automobile came, we changed the appearance and trimming of our Driving Lamp and offered it for use on automobiles. Ever since that time this has been the standard type of construction for Automobile Lamps. We sold these lamps abroad and the French manufacturers imitated our lamp almost exactly."

"Sterling Jr." Side Lamps
1900 – 1914.

Height: 13".
5/8" wick, burned kerosene, 20 candlepower;
6 volt electric bulb, also 20 candlepower.
Front lens, 4 3/8"; side lens, 4 3/8";
ruby jewel lens, 1".
Finish: polished brass, nickel-plate, black
nickel-plate, or painted.

Used on both carriages and
automobiles.

Rare.

Kerosene Burner Only.

From 1890 to 1930 Dietz made many
styles of auto headlights– including
Orient, Regal, Union, No. 673, No.
1065, No. 554. They were very much
alike in form. The finishes varied:
japanned black; japanned black with
silver-plated copper reflectors; solid
brass, polished with silver-plated copper
reflectors; solid brass, silver plated all
over. The Ideal and Octo, shown next,
are typical of later headlights.

Combination Kerosene and Electric.

Ideal Lantern
1915 – 1925.

Height: 13 5/8".
5/8" wick, 20 candlepower.
Cold blast.
Finish: polished brass; special finish to
order, black nickel-plate or nickel-plate.

Plain or Fresnel lens with reflector
behind to focus light; plus 1 1/2" rear
ruby lens (to be seen from rear when
lamp was hung on the side of the auto).

Common.

Octo Driving Lantern
1914 – 1930.

Height: 9 3/4".
5/8" wick, 20 candlepower.
Red 2 1/4" rear lens.
Cold blast.
Finish: painted black, with brass rim around hinged door giving access to burner.

Common.

Trolley and Locomotive Headlights
1880 – 1930.

Dead flame.
14", 16", 18", 20", and 23" lens.

Note the lens sizes. Some of these were very large lanterns. These are typical, with slight variations, of the locomotive and streetcar lights manufactured during this period, and illustrate about a quarter of the many styles offered.

All styles are very rare.

No. 998.

Semaphore Streetcar Light
Height: 10".

No. 560 Streetcar Light
Height: 8" and 10".

No. 1395.

Round Case Streetcar Light
Height: 19" high.

Kelly Lamp Company

Founded in 1856 by James H. Kelly, this small company was located at Furnace and Mill streets in Rochester, New York. It manufactured lanterns of the dead-flame type, mainly railroad lanterns and locomotive

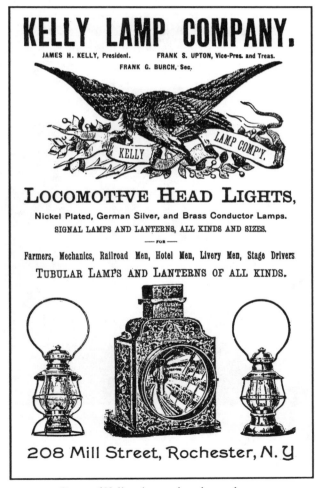

Cover of Kelly sales catalog, date unknown.

headlamps (i.e., lanterns used as headlights). From 1888 to 1897, Kelly included hot-blast tubular lanterns in its sales line. Since it presumably did not have rights to Irwin's patent for this type of lantern, but had no patent violations brought against it, it probably contracted with the Steam Gauge and Lantern Company of Syracuse, New York, as a supplier, since the latter did have the West Coast patent rights for the lanterns. Kelly apparently went out of business after 1897. He died in January 1900. (From 1894 to 1920, Kelly's son, J. H. Kelly, Jr., ran a lantern company in Rochester, New York, called the Rochester Headlight Works. Nothing more is known about him.)

Lanterns from the Kelly Lamp Company are marked "J. H. Kelly, Rochester," often on the underside of the lantern base or font, as shown in the photograph below. The other photograph is of an 1866 Kelly dead-flame lantern from a fire engine. A few other pictures of Kelly lanterns are shown on the sales catalog page, the only piece of Kelly advertising or Kelly lantern illustration that has been located to date. All Kelly lanterns are very rare.

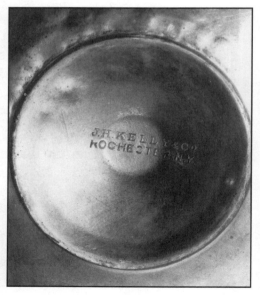

F. Mayrose and Company

In 1857, Ferdinand Mayrose was listed in the St. Louis, Missouri, city directory as a candle molder and maker of Britannia tableware. The business must have flourished because by 1866 he was listed as F. Mayrose and Company, Lanternmakers, at 192 South 4th Street, and in 1867 as F. Mayrose and Company, manufacturers of railroad lamps and lanterns, at 733 South 4th Street. Such listings, with slight changes, continued until 1903, when the company apparently went out of business.

Many companies tried to copy Irwin's patented hot-blast lantern in their own products. F. Mayrose was one such company and consequently, the subject of extended legal action for patent violation by Dietz, which by then owned the eastern and mid-western rights to the patent. The outcome of the litigation is unknown.

The Mayrose lantern that gave rise to this lawsuit is shown here. It does not appear to be a hot-blast lantern, since the side tubes were not fastened to the top of the lantern. Rather, it seems a hybrid hot- cold-blast lantern, because air to the flame was drawn down the side tubes. However, the air was warm, not cold, and taken from a small box fastened to the side of the lantern top (arrow). This air was not directed from the flame, as in a hot blast or from an open air cavity, as in a cold blast. The lantern shown is an unusual design and has a bull's-eye lens. The patent date on its top is "4/22/1871." This and other Mayrose lanterns are very rare.

Ca. 1871 Mayrose lantern.

Chicago Manufacturing Company

Located at 43 and 45 Franklin Street in Chicago, Illinois, this company, which was established in the early 1850s, began manufacturing Irwin's hot-blast lanterns under license from him in 1868. In 1873, Chicago Manufacturing was bought by Dennis and Wheeler.

No original product illustrations for this company were found except for the Champion Conductor's Lantern shown on their letterhead (shown on page 125), which also lists lanterns available from Chicago Manufacturing in 1869, as follows:

No. 0 and No. 1 Tubular.

No. 2 and No. 3 Tubular Mill Lamp.

No. 4 Street Lamp.

No. 5 Beauty (brass) and No. 6 Beauty (German Silver)

No. 7 Champion (conductor)

No. 8 Champion (German Silver), (style shown on the letterhead).

No. 9 Champion (Fancy Tin)

Railroad Coach Lamps.

No. 10 R.R.S.G. with Blower globe or moulded globe.

No. 10 R.R.D.G. with blown or moulded, ruby or green globe.

Railroad Bull's-eye Tail Light.

Marine Port and Starboard Lanterns.

Marine Lamps and Lanterns (various).

Firemen's Lanterns.

Police Lanterns.

Hack Lamps.

"RRSG" stands for railroad single- or double-guard lantern.

A hack lamp is a carriage lamp.

This letter is interesting for another reason besides these illustrations. It is addressed to Irwin, inventor and holder of the hot-blast lantern patent, and mentions Smith. Presumably this is the A. G. Smith who was soon to enter into partnership with R. E. Dietz. Perhaps Smith was, sub rosa, negotiating with the Chicago Manufacturing Company over the West Coast rights to the Irwin patent, which Chicago Manufacturing held at this time. Or perhaps J. S. Dennis was also doing some negotiating, since a new company, Dennis and Wheeler, was founded at about that time.

The reference in the lower left to a "new" lantern is, of course, the hot blast. Lanterns from this company are very rare. It is not known how they were marked. Look for the company name or initials on the bell, or the font, or even under the base, and for the lantern names listed here.

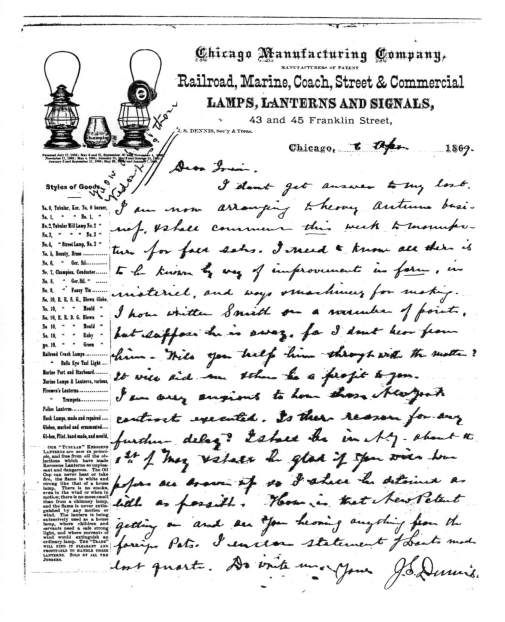

Dennis and Wheeler

Dennis and Wheeler was established as "marine lantern and light manufacturers" in Chicago, Illinois, in 1867. It made other marine equipment and hardware as well. In 1873, it bought the Chicago Manufacturing Company, which had in 1868 begun producing hot-blast lanterns under patent rights granted to it for the West Coast by John Irwin, the patent holder. In 1881, a syndicate headed by Colonel E. S. Jenney bought out Dennis and Wheeler and its products and equipment, using these to help them establish the Steam Gauge and Lantern Company in Rochester, New York.

Old Dennis and Wheeler advertisements indicate that its lanterns were particularly used on rock outcroppings on Lake Michigan waterways, rivers, and canals, as buoy lights. Selling in the Midwest would, of course, have violated the patent, since Dennis and Wheeler had only the West Coast rights.

No original illustrations have been located for Dennis and Wheeler lanterns. They were marked "Dennis and Wheeler." One of their general use, dead-flame lanterns seen by the author had this marking stamped on the bell. Another, a marine lantern, bore the marking on a small brass label affixed to the upper side area of the lantern. (This latter lantern looked similar to the Dietz Marine Lantern of 1888 shown on page 94.) Lanterns from this company are very rare.

D. D. Miller

The D. D. Miller factory operated at 190 Water Street in New York City from 1870 to sometime in the 1920s. It made high- quality dead-flame brass or copper lanterns. Some were of silver or gold or both. It also made excellent-quality, very artistic cut-glass globes. It was unusual for lantern

manufacturers to make their own globes, but these were not ordinary globes, anymore than were their lanterns. The elegant globes were made to match the elegant lanterns. Much of Miller's lantern output went for the fire engines used in parades. In those days, many fire companies had a "parade" engine, beautifully outfitted and decorated, and other more utilitarian engines with which they actually fought fires.

The photograph at left and those on the following page show some D. D. Miller lanterns. Miller lanterns are very rare. They are marked on the bottom "D. D. Miller, Manufacturer, 190 Water St., New York."

Examples of Miller lanterns in the American Museum of Firefighting
in Hudson, New York.

Manufacturer's markings on underside of base.

Nail City Lantern Company/Wheeling Stamping Company

The Nail City Lantern Company was established by Archibald Woods Paull, Sr., in 1877 on Water Street in Wheeling, West Virginia. It

Front page of 1937 Sales Catalog.

employed approximately 50 people at that time, and its principal product was a double-globe dead-flame lantern. (This double-globe lantern probably had a chimney within a globe. See p. 23.)

In 1897, the company was reorganized by Archibald Woods Paull, Jr., and incorporated, its name being changed to the Wheeling Stamping Company. By then, its main products were kerosene lanterns and burners.

By 1895, this company's lantern sales were so well established that R. E. Dietz drafted a proposal to purchase the company. (He estimated that annual production at Nail City was 15,000 dozen lanterns.) It is unclear whether Dietz actually made an offer at this time, but he took another survey in 1899, by which time lantern production was estimated at 16,000 dozen annually. In 1946, Dietz finally did buy the lantern division of the Wheeling Stamping Company. The remaining divisions are still operating in Wheeling, manufacturing collapsible metal tubes and plastic products.

Lanterns made by the Nail City Lantern Company are marked "Nail City" and are very rare. Lanterns made by the Wheeling Stamping Company are marked "Paull's Leader" and are common.

No. 220 Ezy-Lit
1920 – 1946.

Height: 14 3/4"; base diameter: 8 3/4".
No. 2 burner, 1 " wick.
Clear or red globes.
32-oz. font, 45-hour burning time.
Cold blast.
Finish: bright tin or painted green.

Suitable for use on trucks or trailers.

Common.

No. 230 Cold Blast
1920 – 1946.

Height: 11 1/2"; base diameter: 7".
No. O burner, 5/8" wick.
Clear or red globes.
16-oz. font, 30-hour burning time.
Finish: bright tin or painted red.

Common.

No. 250 (not shown)

Similar to the 230, but with a larger,
60-hour font.
Clear, ruby, or green globes.
Cold blast.

Common.

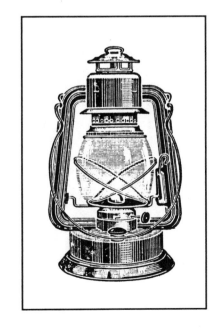

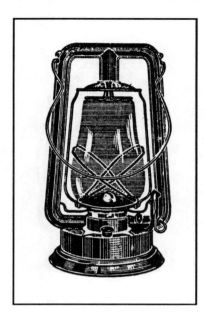

No. 140 Regal
1920 – 1946.

Height: 13 3/4"; base diameter: 7 3/4".
No. O burner, 5/8: wick.
Clear, red, green or blue globes.
16-oz. font, 30-hour burning time.
Hot blast.
Finish: painted red.

Designed for the construction trade, roadwork or railway repair service.

Common: with red globes.

Very rare: green or blue globes.

No. 180 Leader
1920 – 1946.

Height: 15"; base diameter: 8 1/2".
No. 2 burner, 1" wick.
Clear or red globes.
32-oz. font, 45-hour burning time.
Cold blast.
Finish:: bright tin or painted green.

Sales brochures recommended it for farm, camping, and boating.

Common.

Steam Gauge and Lantern Company

In 1881, Colonel E. S. Jenney, an attorney, formed a syndicate with sufficient capital to buy or control the Irwin lantern patents and to purchase the companies of one or both of the two manufacturers then legitimately making hot-blast lanterns: R. E. Dietz and Dennis and Wheeler. (One of the major investors in this syndicate was C. T. Ham, who later started his own lantern company.) Colonel Jenney secured from Dennis and Wheeler, which had the hot blast manufacturing rights for the western United States, an option to purchase its business. He then tried to buy R. E. Dietz, which held the rights to the East Coast and the Midwest. The offer was, after some consideration, rejected by Dietz.

Picture of Steam Gauge and Lantern Company Factory, Ca. 1881, showing its location at the Genesee Falls.

The Jenney syndicate went ahead with the Dennis and Wheeler purchase, moving all its equipment, in the fall of 1881, to Rochester, New York, where the Genesee Falls provided cheap power and where labor also was available. There, with a paid-in capital of $250,000, the Steam Gauge and Lantern Company was started.

Since the Irwin patent contract allowed only one factory on the East Coast, and Dietz already had that, the Jenney syndicate, in order to locate its factory at Rochester, first had to obtain permission from R. E. Dietz. For granting this privilege, Dietz secured a substantial reduction in royalties paid to Colonel Jenney, who now held the West Coast Irwin patent for selling in that territory.

Steam Gauge and Lantern proved to be a strong company and for a time earned good profits, paying the stockholders substantial dividends. However, a disastrous fire in November 1888 totally destroyed its factory, killing 35 employees. The company moved to Syracuse, New York, that same year and continued to manufacture lanterns there until 1897. In the summer of 1897, it was bought by R. E. Dietz. (Presumably, the two companies had been on friendly terms before the merger. The author found an old price list in the Dietz archives, dated June 1883 and signed by both the Steam Gauge and Lantern Company and R. E. Deitz, in which each agreed to fix prices on lanterns that were similar in model or style to those of the other company.)

The Steam Gauge and Lantern Company designed an interesting burner attachment called, perhaps because of its resemblance to a little hat, the Stetson Safety Attachment. Its purpose was to lock the burner in place with small lock-in tags, eliminating the nightmarish problem of fire from spilled lantern fuel when a lantern fell over, broke, and ignited the fuel. (Burner tops were usually held in place by the globe plate. If the globe broke, the burner could fall out, spilling and firing whatever combustible material was in the font. Stable and house fires often resulted. The Stetson attachment kept the burner from falling out if the globe broke.)

Lanterns from this company are very rare. They are marked on the top of the font "Steam Gauge and Lantern" or "SG & L Co."

No. O Safety Tubular Lantern
1888 – 1897.

No. 1 burner, 5/8" wick.
Hot blast.
Finish: lantern, tin; reflector, shiny nickel
inside, black paint outside.

Rare.

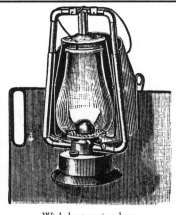

With lantern in place.

Dash board reflector attachment
designed to fit most tubular lanterns.

No. O and No. 2 (not shown)
Tubular Lanterns
1881 – 1888.

Height: 15".
No. 1 lantern had a No. 1 burner, and a
5/8" wick.
No. 2 lantern had a No. 2 burner and a 1"
wick.
Hot blast.
Finish: bright tin.

These were manufactured in Steam
Gauge and Lantern's Rochester, New
York factory, which burned down in
1888. The wire globe lifter on these
early models distinguished them from the
later No. O. A removable, horizontal tin
shade reflector was available, for both
sizes, to reflect light downward. These
lanterns also were made from 1888 to
1897 at the Syracuse factory, with a solid
sheet metal globe lifter (shown).

Very rare: both models.

No. O Tubular Lantern.

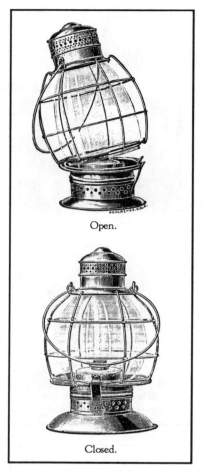

Open.

Closed.

No. 7 Lake & River Lantern
1881 – 1897.

Burned kerosene only.
6" x 6" government globe.
Dead flame.
Finish: bright tin or choice of paint colors.

Manufactured to government standards, and advertised as being the "new government pattern." Hinged at font for easy access. A marine lantern.

Very rare.

U.S.L.H.E. Safety Lantern
1886 – 1897.

Height: 15 1/4"; base diameter, 9".
No. 1 burner, 5/8" wick.
Hot blast.

The standard government lantern, used to light buoys, etc. The "U.S.L.H.E." stands for United States Light House Engineers.

Very rare.

U.S. Safety Brass Lantern
1886 – 1897.

No. O burner, 3/8" wick.
Hot blast.
Finish: brass.

A well-made, polished lantern
for household use.

Rare.

No. 2 Railroad Lantern
1888 – 1897.

Burned animal fat (lard oil).
Dead flame.

Similar to the Dietz No. 39 Standard
Lantern (see p. 95).

Very rare.

Vesta Railroad Lantern
1888 – 1897.

Burned animal fat (lard oil).
Dead flame.

Had a glass oil font, which no other
railroad lantern had as standard issue.

Very rare.

No. 39 Wire Bottom Lantern
1888 – 1897.

Dead flame.

Similar to the Dietz. No. 39 Vulcan Railroad, 1888 – 1912, (see p. 96). Although marked SG & L Co., they may have bought this from Dietz.

Rare.

No. 47 Commercial Lantern
1888 – 1897.

Dead flame.
Single guard only.

Similar to the No. 43 Dietz (see p. 96).

Very rare.

No. 43 Commercial Lantern. (not shown)
1888 – 1897

Similar to the No. 47 but with single or double guard.

Very rare.

No. 13 Safety Dash Lantern
1888 – 1897.

No. 1 burner, 5/8" wick.
Hot blast.
Finish: tin, painted black.

This square font model held enough oil to burn 16 hours. Also made with round font which burned 12 hours (not shown).

Very rare: square font.

Rare: round font.

Used as carriage and early automobile lantern.

No. O Safety Tubular Hood Reflector Lantern
1888 – 1897.

No. 1 burner, 5/8" wick.
5" silvered-glass reflector and
nickel-plated hood.
Hot blast.

Used as carriage and early automobile lantern.

Rare.

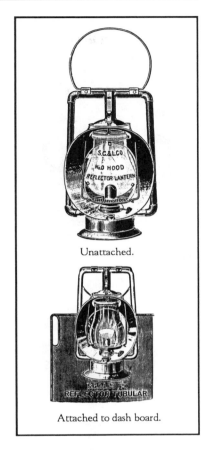

Unattached.

Attached to dash board.

Tricolored Trackwalker or Inspector's Lantern
1882 – 1897.

4" reflector.
Dead flame.

Turning handle could rotate interior cylinder holding different-color glass and lens. Lens could show red, green, or clear.

Very rare.

Rear Signal Lamp for a Train
1884 – 1897.

Dead flame.
Large, permanent bracket.

Very rare.

Savage or Engineer's Lantern
1881 – 1897.

Dead flame.
Finish: brass or tin.

A compact lantern, for use inside the engine compartment.

Very rare.

Square Signal Light
1881 – 1897.

Dead flame.
Finish: bright tin, painted black.

Rare.

A Selection of Brass and Nickel-plate Conductor's Lanterns
1881 – 1897.

All of these are dead-flame lanterns and all are very rare.

No. 39 is a standard size used on railroads; with a fire lantern ring on top, it is the railroad fireman's lantern, not the conductor's. No. 1 was sold with two-color glass globes (shown).

No. 4 is a small lantern 8" high.

Note similarity to Dietz selections (see p. 103). Some of these may have been bought from Dietz.

No. 39. Conductor's.

No. 39. Fireman's–Ring in Top.

No. 1. Conductor's.

No. 2. Conductor's.

No. 5. Conductor's.

No. 8. Conductor's.

No. 4. Conductor's.

No. 3. Conductor's.

No. 6. Conductor's.

No. 2 Signal Lamp.

No. 3 Signal Lamp.

No. 2 and No. 3 Tubular Square Bridge Signal Lamps
1886 – 1897.

Height: No. 2, approximately 15";
No. 3, approximately 25".
No. 2: 7" silvered-glass reflector;
No. 3: 12" silvered-glass reflector.
No internal chimney.
Available with any colored glass required.
Hot blast.

Rare.

"These lamps are arranged with Colored Glass in the front and in the sides, with Silvered Glass Reflector in the back of the lamp, and powerful Kerosene Burners, made especially for our Tubular Lamps. The body of the lamp is made of galvanized iron – strong and durable, with extra heavy bails and with rings on the bottom for attaching the lamp to the guy rope. The lamps are also made for four lights of glass instead of three, if desired."

Note that "light" as used here means "pane" of glass. This is an English and early American usage.

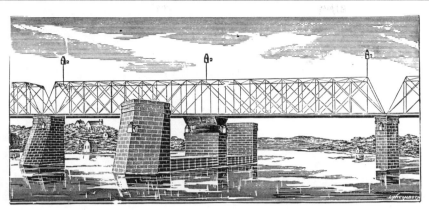

CLOSED.   No. 1.

OPEN,   No. 2.

Draw Bridge arranged with Tubular Square Bridge Signal Lamps in use as signals.

Cut No. 1, illustrating the Draw-Bridge closed, shows the Tubular Bridge Signal Lamps having ruby and green glass on opposite sides. The ruby lights in line with the river, and the green lights in line with the track, indicate that the bridge is closed.

In Cut No. 2 the ruby lights in line with the track, and the green lights in line with the river, indicate that the bridge is open.

The lamps on the abutments have ruby glass on three sides, and are used as danger signals indicating the location of the abutments."

C. T. Ham Manufacturing Company

Prior to opening his own factory, C. T. Ham was involved with a number of lantern manufacturers as a lantern inventor and as a board member. Thus, when he founded his company in 1887, in Rochester, New York, he was well acquainted with lantern production. As part of his business, he manufactured for other companies. (For example, old billing statements to the Ohio Lantern Company indicate that Ham shipped 693 dozen railroad lanterns, at a cost of 47 cents each. There were many other such billings, including large shipments to the Buhl Stamping Company and the Nail City Lantern Company.) Ham offered good-quality brass hot- and cold-blast lanterns — a broad line to the general public, as well as more specialized lines.

R. E. Dietz was impressed with this company and offered to buy its entire plant, machinery, tools, dies, patents, and goodwill. Included in the proposed deal was all its "street lamp, railroad and other lantern business." The honorary title of vice-president and a salary of $4,000 a year were offered to C. T. Ham, and a $1,000 annual salary to Ham's son, George Ham, who was part owner. The takeover did not go through. There is some correspondence in 1897 and again in 1910, between Dietz and Ham, but nothing to indicate why, about 1914, the company closed down.

No illustrations have been found to date for Ham lanterns. Their dead-flame lanterns were not distinctive, but their hot-blast and cold-blast lanterns can be distinguished by a lower bell assembly which extended out to the side tubes as a support.

Most Ham lanterns are marked "C. T. Ham Co.," typically on the top but sometimes on the side. All are very rare.

Defiance Lantern and Stamping Company

In 1900, William C. Embury, a designer and inventor, founded the Defiance Lantern and Stamping Company in Rochester, New York, with money borrowed from a few wealthy investors. In 1917, pressure from the board of directors, the reasons for which are unclear, caused Embury to resign. He then established the Embury Lantern Manufacturing Company in Warsaw, New York. In 1935, thanks to good growth and management, Embury was able to purchase and absorb the Defiance Lantern and Stamping Company. He proceeded to close it and to move most of its equipment to his Warsaw factory.

Defiance manufactured mainly railroad-type (i.e., similar to the No. 39 style), dead-flame lanterns until about 1918. These are easy to recognize because of their distinctive twisted-wire guards. Unfortunately, this wire could unravel, catch on nearby objects, and make the lantern difficult to use. It became necessary to scrap the line. Defiance then began to manufacture railway lanterns similar to those of other manufacturers, marking them with the Defiance name. However, its product line after 1910 moved more toward the contractor and general public, offering hot- and cold-blast lanterns with a unique and easily recognized globe guard and wire lift system (see, e.g., its No. 2 Dash Lamp). The following list, from a 1926 Defiance catalog, suggests the styles offered that year.

Defiance lanterns are marked "Defiance" on top. Defiance lanterns made before 1910, identifiable by their twisted-wire guards, are rare.

No. 0 Perfect Tubular Lift.

No. 0 Perfect Lift Dash Lamp (2 burner sizes).

No. 3 Hanging Lamp.

No. 3 Street Lamp.

No. 2 Triangular Lantern

No. 200 Triumph Lantern.

No. 1 Small Rival Lantern.

No. 2 Large Rival Lantern.

The Jewel Driving Lamp (a tubular dash type).

No. 1 Station Lamp.

No. 2 Station Lamp.

No. 3 Station Lamp (square type).

Cover from 1926 Defiance Catalog.

No. 39 Lantern
1918 – 1935.

Height: 10".
Available with lard oil, signal
oil, or kerosene burner.
Dead flame.

Although marked "Defiance,"
from the details of these lamps
it appears that one model was
bought from Dietz (as shown,
but with the wick adjuster
inside the globe) and one model
from Adams & Westlake.

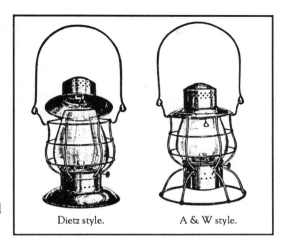

Dietz style.   A & W style.

Rare: both models.

The Little Gem Lantern
1901 – 1930s.

Firefly burner.
Dead flame.
Finish: brass.

Identical size and similar to Dietz's Baby
Lantern (p. 107), but has a bail rather than a
chain on top.

For skating and for general household use.
Skaters used these lanterns to light areas of
the ice pond, leaving their shoes by the
lantern when they changed to skates.

Common.

Defiance Searchlight
1905 – 1930s.

No. 2 burner, 1" wick.
11 3/4" reflector.
Bull's-eye lens was molded into the globe.
Cold blast.
Finish: blue japanned.

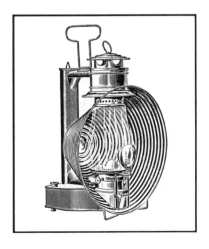

A larger model, made from 1919 – 1930,
was 15" high, with a 12" reflector and
35-hour font, finished in bright red.

Common: both models.

No. 1 Jewel Lantern
1905 – 1935.

Height: 12 1/2"; 5/8" wick.
Ruby, blue, white, or green globes.
Cold blast.
Finish: bright tin.

Common.

No. 2 Defiance Dash Lantern
1919 – 1935.

Height: 14 3/4".
No. 2 burner, 1" wick.
Bull's-eye lens molded into the globe.
Cold blast.
Finish: painted red.

A carriage or early automobile lantern.

Common.

The Peerless Lantern
1901 – 1914.

No. 1 burner, 5/8" wick.
Sangster oil pot.
Dead flame.

Globe was removed by sliding the circular top of the upright guard out of notch on lantern top. Available with or without a globe guard.

Rare.

Side Reflector Lamp
1901 – 1910.

No. 2 burner, 1" wick.
5" silvered-glass reflector.
Cold blast.
Finish: plain, unpolished tin
or japanned blue.

Rare.

A similar model, painted red, was made from 1910 – 1935. It had a 35-hour font and was distinguished from the one shown by horizontal crimp marks on the back, which came from strengthening the metal frame by compression during manufacture.

Common.

No. O Regular Tubular Lantern
1901 – 1930s.

No. 1 burner, 5/8" wick.
Red or plain globes.
Hot blast.
Finish: bright tin.

Common.

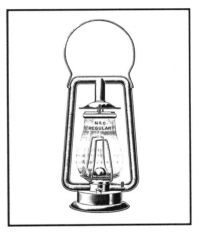

No. O Inspector's Lamp
1910 – 1930s.

Height 15".
No. O burner, 5/8" wick.
5" reflector, 6" deep.
Hot blast.
Finish: heavy tin.

Common.

Embury Manufacturing Company

In 1917, William C. Embury started the Embury Manufacturing Company, specializing in utility, contractor, and highway warning lanterns. In 1953, the company was acquired by the R. E. Dietz Company, which continued to operate it in Warsaw under the Embury name until the 1960s, when it was closed down.

One of Embury's lanterns, the Traffic Guard Lantern, produced from 1945 to 1962, was directed at the same market as the Dietz Night Watch Lantern. However, Embury's sales were far greater than Dietz's for this product, so when Dietz bought Embury, it replaced its lantern with Embury's. That is, the lantern was taken out of the Embury catalog, even though Embury was still operating, and put in the Dietz catalog, still marked "Embury." The popularity of the Traffic Guard Lantern with contractors was so strong that it may have been a major motivation for Dietz's buyout of Embury.

Red globes are very common on Embury products because of their intended users. For the same reason, many Embury lanterns can be found with one of the following inscriptions either on the top of the bell or on the top of the font. These inscriptions were taken from the stamped plates used to make the lanterns. Many other inscriptions, more than for most other companies, can be found on Embury lanterns, but these are the most common.

Stolen from State Highway Dept.	Dept. of Public Works.
Street Dept.	DW&P.
Dept of Parks.	Prop. S&W Board
Dept. of Public Utilities.	PWD Water Works.

No. 0R Air Pilot
Mid 1940s – 1962.

Height: 13 1/8"; 5/8" wick.
Red or clear globes.
Hot blast.
Finish: painted metallic green.

Very common.

No. 350R Little Supreme
Mid 1940s – 1962.

Height: 12 1/4"; 5/8" wick.
Red or clear globes.
Cold blast.
Finish: painted metallic green.

For farm use.

Common.

A similar lantern, the **No. 2 Camlox** (not shown), had a copper font, and its upper section was painted black.

Rare.

No. 2R Air Pilot
Mid 1940s – 1962.

Height: 13 1/2"; 7/8" wick.
Red or clear globes.
Cold blast.
Finish: painted metallic green.

Very common.

No. 1R Little Air Pilot
Mid 1940s – 1962.

Height: 11 3/4"; 5/8" wick.
Red or clear globes.
Cold blast.
Finish: painted metallic green.

Very common.

No. 40R Traffic-Guard
1945 – 1962.

Height: 7 3/4"; 1/4" round felt wick.
Clear, red, amber, green, and blue globes.
Dead flame.
Finish: painted red or yellow.

Burned 72 hours on pint of kerosene or signal oil.

Very common: red and clear globes.

Rare: amber, green or blue globes.

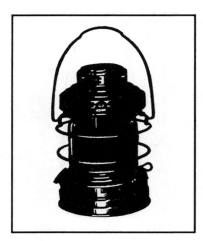

No. 225R Luck-E-Light
Mid 1940s – 1962.

Height: 8 7/8"; base diameter: 5 3/4".
Red or clear globes.
Dead flame.
Finish: painted red or yellow.

Both this and the No. 40R Lanterns were construction marker lights.

Very common.

All these Embury lanterns are shown with colored globes.

Armspear Manufacturing Company

Also known as the Railroad Signal Lamp and Lantern Company, Armspear operated from the late 19th century into the 1920s and had its main office at 447 West 53rd Street in New York City. It eventually had offices in Chicago, Boston, Washington, and Richmond, Virginia. It apparently went out of business in the mid-1920s.

Besides the lanterns shown in the following pages, Armspear manufactured railroad engine lights, caboose rear lights, signal lights, and other railroad lanterns. The illustrations shown here are from the period 1890 – 1914.

In 1906, Armspear advertised a new design for railroad lanterns. These were heavy-steel, straight-body railway lamps, similar in style to Adlake's but with a side door that allowed top- or bottom-draft ventilation. The lamp could be used in all climates and locations, because the design controlled air flow through the lantern and greatly reduced the condensation (heat in summer, frost buildup in winter) that caused rust and rapid corrosion in the lantern.

ARMSPEAR
MANUFACTURING
COMPANY

MAIN OFFICE AND FACTORY

447–451 WEST FIFTY-THIRD STREET

NEW YORK CITY

BRANCH OFFICES

BOSTON   CHICAGO   WASHINGTON

Cover of Armspear Sales Catalog, date unknown.

No. 3 Lantern
Ca. 1907 – 1920.

Shown with colored globe.
Dead flame.

Available with one or two guards, and with any style and size burner required, it could burn lard oil as well as kerosene.

Common: all styles.

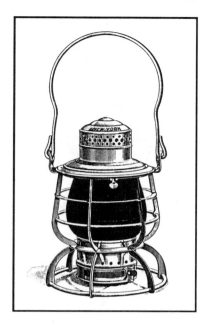

Gauge Lamps

Dead flame.

These were not lanterns. Usually made of brass or nickel-plate, these small lamps were mounted above engine-room dials to light them, so steam pressure could be read by the engineer. They came from the factory in clear glass, but they can be found with painted globes. The engineers painted them to dull their light so that it was less distracting in the small space of the engine room.

Rare: painted or unpainted.

The Gem
Ca. 1907.

Had a spring globe adjuster, and a hinged top.
Dead flame.

Font screwed into the base from below.
The Pet (not shown) was similar, but smaller.

Very rare: both models.

The Railway Queen
Ca. 1907.

Dead flame.
Similar to the Gem, but with an open (skeleton) bottom.

This and the Gem lantern, although labeled Armspear, probably were made by Adlake. Both were conductor's lanterns.

Very rare.

No. 4 Lantern
1880 – 1910.

Dead flame.
Similar to the Gem, but cheaper in construction.

Rare.

No. 39 Lantern
1900 – 1920.

Sangster spring oil pot.
Dead flame
Finish: brass.

Labeled Armspear, but probably made by Dietz.

Common.

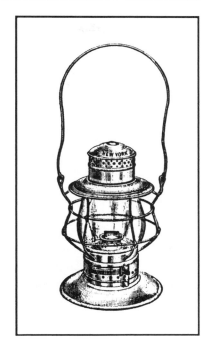

Fireman's Lantern
1880 – 1910.

Available with signal oil burner, kerosene burner, or spring candlestick holder.
Dead flame

Top covered with a hood that kept water from extinguishing the flame.

Very rare.

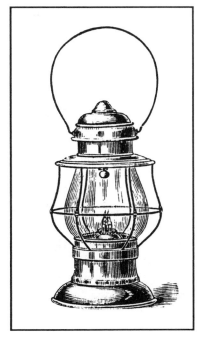

Adams and Westlake Limited

This company was founded by John McGregor Adams and John Crerar, who had come to Chicago in 1856 as salesmen for a New York City company. Aware of the rapid growth of population and development of railroads in the western United States, they decided to form their own business. Called Adams, Crerar and Company, it was established in 1857 to produce and sell supplies for contractors and railroad builders, including hardware and metalware as well as lanterns. By 1865, the company had become so successful that it needed its own factory. Erected on Franklin Street between Ontario and Ohio streets, this factory was destroyed in the great Chicago fire of 1871. It was immediately rebuilt in 1872. Because of expanding business, the company merged with one that Adams and Crerar already owned, the Union Brass Manufacturing Company, which had been incorporated in 1869.

In 1863, William Westlake had come to Chicago from Milwaukee. He was a coppersmith and a locomotive engineer, and the inventor of a removable globe lantern. With patents for this, and a lot of expertise, he organized a new company called Cross, Dane, and Westlake, to produce both this lantern and oil-burning headlights also of his invention. His Michigan Avenue factory also fell victim to the great fire of 1871. In 1872, the firm was reorganized as Dane, Westlake, and Covert, and a new factory was built at Franklin and Lake streets in Chicago. This building had a "fine and commodious store" open to the public for retail sales. The initial capital investment was $100,000, and 120 men and boys were employed, with a weekly payroll of $1,300. The estimated annual production was valued at $350,000. Sometime in 1873, a legal action was brought against this company for violation of the John Irwin lantern patents. This probably created financial difficulties and contributed to the company's closing in early 1874.

On October 21, 1874, it reopened with a new name, Adams and Westlake, with Adams as president, Dane as vice-president, and Westlake

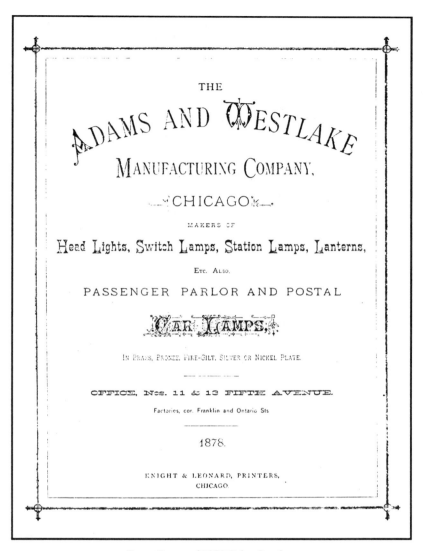

THE

ADAMS AND WESTLAKE

MANUFACTURING COMPANY,

CHICAGO.

MAKERS OF

Head Lights, Switch Lamps, Station Lamps, Lanterns,

ETC. ALSO,

PASSENGER PARLOR AND POSTAL

CAR LAMPS,

IN BRASS, BRONZE, FIRE-GILT, SILVER OR NICKEL PLATE.

OFFICE, Nos. 11 & 13 FIFTH AVENUE.

Factories, cor. Franklin and Ontario Sts

1878.

KNIGHT & LEONARD, PRINTERS,
CHICAGO.

Front Cover of 1878 Sales Catalog.

as secretary. This company purchased the assets of Dane, Westlake, and Covert as well as the assets of the Chicago Railway Lantern Company. The production equipment and products from these companies were transferred to the Union Brass Manufacturing Company building. Here the firm made railway lanterns, train headlights, oil lighting fixtures for railcars, signal lamps, and related equipment. In 1884, in response to increased trade, an additional plant was built on Ontario Street in Chicago.

In 1887, the Union Brass Manufacturing Company and Adams and Westlake were merged, under the Adams and Westlake name. The new company's product line was now diversified and included brass beds, stove floor mats, bicycles, cameras, window sashes, and curtains, as well as lanterns. In 1899, the window shade division of Adams and Westlake joined with the Forsyth Brothers Company, curtain manufacturers, to form a new division called the Curtain Supply Company. In 1923, this division moved from Chicago to a new plant in Elkhart, Indiana.

By late 1923, Adams and Westlake's old buildings in Chicago had become outdated and inefficient to operate. The decision was made to move all production equipment, as well as the company's offices, to Elkhart, Indiana, where it already had an office. In 1927, the firm built a new plant which today covers an area of ten acres. This has been its headquarters ever since. The company still manufactures hardware and related items, but not lanterns.

From 1899 to the 1930s, Adlake produced a "Non-sweating Balanced Draft Ventilation" system for most of its lamps and lanterns. Because the bodies of the lamps and lanterns were made of steel, corrosion was a major problem, which this system was designed to overcome. Thanks to the increased air flow inside the lamp body, frost or ice buildup was no longer a problem in winter, and moisture (sweating) in summer was eliminated as well. Lamps and lanterns that do not have the "non-sweating" system probably predate the 1899 time period in design, but not necessarily in production.

In 1907, Adlake started to offer "electric light" attachments to replace existing oil fonts in lamps and lanterns in use, or as an option on new products.

Adlake Lanterns

Although many illustrations have been located for Adlake lanterns, it has been difficult to obtain detailed specifications for them. However, because Adlake's output was so focused on railroad products, some generalizations may be made about the appearance and composition of its lanterns. They were extremely utilitarian, rather similar in most of their styles, and, with the exception of the hand lanterns, usually lacked the grace and variety of lanterns made by manufacturers with a broader market focus.

In style, material, and finish, Adlake lanterns aimed at strength and durability. Because of their intended use, they were as a rule larger and heavier than the product lines of other manufacturers and almost invariably finished in a utilitarian black paint. Their hand lanterns, though, were the standard 10" to 15" high. Again because of their railroad use, these were mostly dead-flame lanterns and burned signal oil, except for an occasional kerosene adaptation. The burners usually were the standard ones for dead-flame lanterns. Many of these lanterns tended to have not globes but all-encompassing steel bodies with one or more openings for large lenses. These latter could be closed, with a sliding steel door, or could be changed in color by one or more methods of inserting colored glass between the lens and the flame.

Adlake lanterns range from rare to very rare. You are most likely to come across them in one of the railroad memorabilia shows held around the country. Because this company specialized so heavily in railway products, the lamp and lantern types, and their functions, are listed in the following pages according to their use by the railways around the 1900s. Some of the illustrations that follow show how these were actually used by early railroad personnel.

On the lamps and lanterns illustrated in the following pages, the mounting clamp is shown, but mounts were sold as a separate item, so the lamps or lanterns you may find will normally not have mounting clamps attached.

Where, in the following pages, "Pre-1899" design is noted, it dates the lantern as 1860s to 1890s. "Post-1889" denotes 20th-century lanterns, used into the 1940s in some areas. The earlier lanterns were marked "Adams and Westlake", usually on the top. Around 1890, this was changed to "Adlake."

Adlake Hand Lanterns

As we noted before, many Adlake lanterns were large and very heavy, usually because they were made as stationary or engine lights. Other, smaller ones, designed as hand lanterns (No. 11 to No. 7 on the next few pages), were only a small part of Adlake's product line. They were used primarily by railroad guards to signal the engineer either from the track or from the rear of the train, or to warn other trains of a problem on the track. Different colored globes had different meanings:

- Red: "Danger. Stop train and await instructions."
- Yellow: "Warning. Go slow. Proceed with caution to the next signal."
- Blue::   "Warning. Men working on tracks or on a nearby stopped train on another line. Proceed with caution."
- Green: "All clear."

Signals also were conveyed by the position in which a hand lantern was held. The next illustrations, taken from the Standard Code of Train Rules issued by the American Railway Association on April 25, 1906, show the meanings of some common lantern positions.

Diagrams of Hand Lamp Signals

Release Air Brakes – Held at arm's
length above the head.

Back – Swung vertically in a circle
across the track.

Proceed – Raised and lowered vertically.

Stop – Swung across the track.

Apply air brakes – Swung
horizontally above the head.

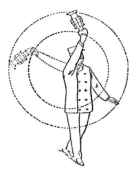

Train has parted – Swung vertically in a
circle at arm's length across the track.

No. 11 Single and Double Wire Guard Lanterns
1880s – 1930s.

No. 1 burner, 5/8" wick, or
No. 2 burner, 1" wick.
Burned signal oil or lard oil.
Finish: bright tin.

Both size burners were available as an option for those who needed a longer burning flame more than a brilliant flame. (The latter was more expensive.)

The No. 1 and No. 2 lanterns were similar, but can be easily distinguished by the outside wick adjuster. The bail lock hook was introduced about 1915.

Single wire guard.
Inside wick adjuster.

Double wire guard.
Outside wick adjuster.

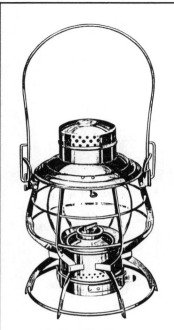

Inside wick adjuster.

No. 11 Adams Steel Guard Lantern
1905 – 1930s.

No. 1 burner, 5/8" wick, or
No. 2 burner, 1" wick.
Burned signal oil, but had a ratchet for
adjusting the wick, which was unusual in an
animal-fat burner.
Finish: bright tin.

After the 1920s this model was made
with a kerosene burner.

These similar lanterns are easily
distinguished by the the outside wick
adjuster.

Common: both models.

The bail-lock hook was introduced about
1915. From 1920 to the 1940s these
lanterns were called **Adlake-Kero** and
had kerosene burners.

Rare: both models.

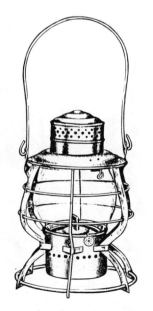

Outside wick adjuster.

No. 39 Double Wire Guard Lanterns
1890 – 1920.

No. 1 burner, 5/8" wick, or
No. 2 burner, 1" wick.
Burned signal oil.
Finish: tin.

These similar lanterns are easily distinguished by the outside wick adjuster. This lantern also was made with a single wire guard. (Not shown.)

The 1878 Adlake catalog lists a No. 39 lantern with a non- adjustable, two-tube burner. This is the earliest mention of a No. 39 lantern, by any company, that the author has found in his research, so perhaps Adlake originated the No. 39 lantern. In any case this style became a standard model for several manufacturers. Adlake No. 39 lanterns were sold to the railroads but not to the general public, so they had signal oil burners rather than kerosene burners.

Rare: all models.

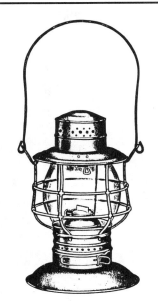

Inside wick adjuster.

Outside wick adjuster.

"The Queen"
Closed Bottom

"The Queen"
Open Bottom

The Queen and The Pullman
1875 – 1910.

Nearly all companies that made lanterns offered these or very similar styles of conductor's lanterns. Many were of high quality, finished in silver or nickel-plated brass.

Very rare: all models.

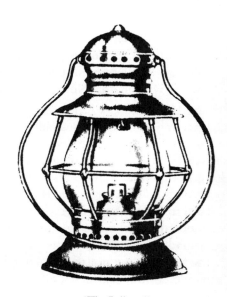

"The Pullman"

No. 40 and No. 7 Steamboat Lanterns
1880s – 1910s.

No. 1 burner, 5/8" wick,
or No. 2 burner, 1" wick.
Burned signal oil.
6" x 6" government globe (see glossary).

The smaller No. 7 lantern was similar to the No. 40. but can be most quickly distinguished from it by its smaller (No. 7) globe size and its bail, which had no hanger indentation.

These hand lanterns were used by steamboat engineers and other marine personnel much as the conductor and guards used them to signal on railroads.

Very rare: both lanterns.

No. 40 Steamboat Lantern

No. 7 Steamboat Lantern

Engine and Tender Signal Lanterns

These lanterns were quite large; heavier and considerably bigger than the hand signal lanterns. The illustrations on this page and the following page indicate where such lanterns were to be displayed on the engine and on the tender (the car behind the locomotive which stored coal, wood, or

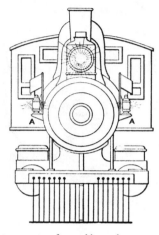

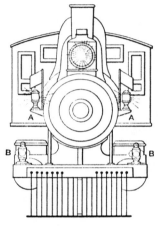

Engine running forward by night as an extra train. White lights and white flags at A A.

Engine running backward by night as an extra train, without cars or at the rear of a train pushing cars. White lights and white flags at A A. Lights at B B, as markers, showing green at side and in direction engine is moving, and red in opposite direction.

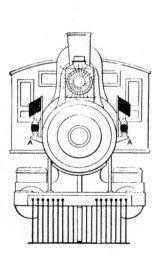

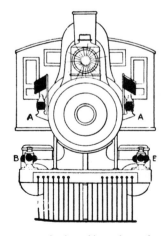

Engine running forward at night displaying signals for a following section. Green lights and green flags at A A.

Engine running backward by night, without cars or at the rear of a train pushing cars and displaying signals for a following section. Green lights and green flags at A A. Lights at B B, as markers, showing green at side and in direction engine is moving and red in opposite direction.

other fuel), in order to give the specific signals recommended by the 1907 Standard Code of Rules. Mounting brackets were attached to the cars in the places where a lantern was to be displayed, holding it in a rigid, stationary position. These lanterns also usually had handles or bails so that they could be lifted out and taken down for cleaning or refueling.

Not only the positions but the various colors displayed by these classification lanterns signaled intentions. The eight classification lanterns (No. 187 to No. 205) shown on pages 170-173, illustrate various ways they stored and displayed colored glass, or some actually had colored lenses or globes. Each different color signaled an intention. For example, that your train was proceeding through a particular point junction.

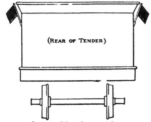

Engine running forward by day, without cars or at the rear of a train pushing cars. Green flags, as markers.

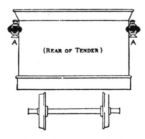

Engine running forward by night, without cars or at the rear of a train pushing cars. Lights at A A, as markers, showing green to the front and side and red to the rear.

Engine running backward by night without cars or at the front of a train pulling cars. White light at A

No. 187 Automatic Engine Classification Lamp
Post-1899 design.

Two 5" or 5 3/8" clear lenses.

Colored-glass (red, green, and white) disks between the lenses and the flame slid up (away) or down (in place) to give different color to the lantern lights.

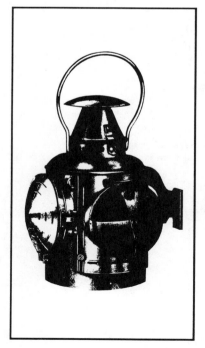

No. 85 Acme Lamp
Post-1899 Design.

Hinged lens caps could be opened for insertion of different glass disks. The colored-glass disks were stored in the side compartment on the exterior of the lamp.

No. 202 Pressed Steel Lamp
Post-1899 design.

*4 1/3", 4 1/2", 5", or 5 3/8" lenses.
Outside wick adjuster.*

Colored-glass slides stored in the side compartment could be removed and placed over the lens to show color desired.

Hinged top opened for ease in cleaning interior.

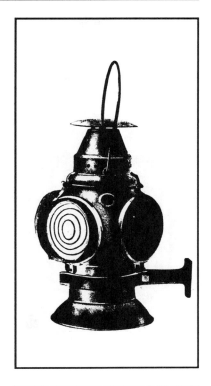

No. 77 Steel Lamp
Post-1899 design.

Colored-glass slides stored in interior pocket inside of lamp could be removed and placed over lens to show color desired.

Hinged top for ease in cleaning interior.

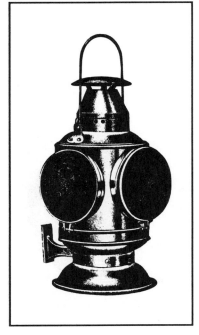

No. 41 Lamp
Pre-1899 design.

Colored- glass slides stored in interior pocket inside of lamp could be removed and placed over lens to show color desired.

No. 42 Lamp
Pre-1899 design.

Lower draft air flow system.

Colored-glass slides, stored in interior pocket inside of lamp could be removed and placed over lens to show color desired.

No. 91 Lamp
Pre-1899 design.

Equipped with one each white and green one-third circle opaque lens. The lenses of this lantern were curved to follow the shape of the lantern body.

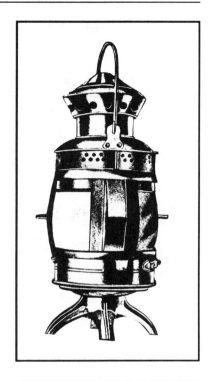

No. 205 Tender Marker Lamp
Post-1899 design.

5" or 5 3/8" clear lens.

Colored-glass disks could be moved up and down over the lens, by means of an exterior lever, to change colors.

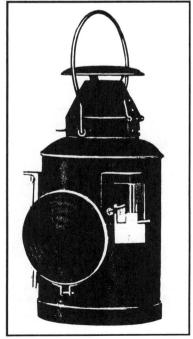

Cupola, Coach, Caboose Marker or Tail Lamps, and Station Platform Lamps

The lamps on the following pages (No. 83 to No. 130), were used in many different ways to signal intentions or special stops or problems. For instance, the lamp on the station platform could signal, with one color, to stop for mail or a special passengers.

On the following pages, 175-181, A, B, C, D, or E indicates where, on the railroad car, a lantern was placed in order to give a specific signal.

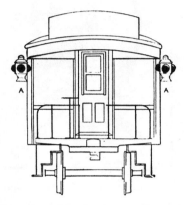

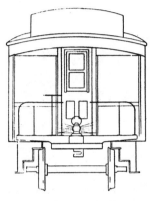

A. Rear of train by night when on siding to be passed by another train. Lights at A A, as markers, showing green toward engine, side and to rear.

B. Passenger cars being pushed by an engine by night. White light on front of leading car.

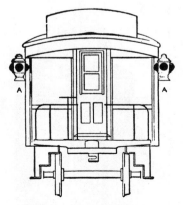

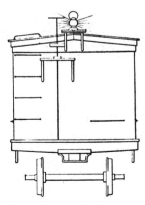

C. Rear of train by night while running. Lights at A A, as markers, showing green toward engine and side and red to rear.

D. Freight cars being pushed by an engine by night. White light on front of leading car.

E. Center rear of caboose.

No. 83 Round Body Tail Lamp

Post-1899 design.

*Unusual size 6 3/4" ruby lens,
and three 5 3/8" green lenses.*

Heavy steel construction.

Signal position A.

No. 78 Steel Marker or Tail Lamp

Post-1899 design.

*Available with one, two, three, or four 5 3/8"
lenses in various colors. Lenses of other sizes
available.*

Hinged top for easy cleaning.

Signal position A or C.

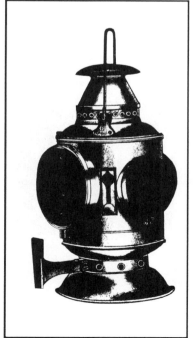

No. 203 Pressed Steel Tail or Marker Lamp
Post-1899 design.

Available with one, two, three, or four 5 3/8" lenses in various colors.

Signal position A or C.

No. 15 Platform and Tail Lamp
Post-1899 design.

8" ruby lens, and a plain white glass, 4 1/2" in diameter on each side. Lighted the rear of a coach or caboose.

Signal position E.

Front view of lantern

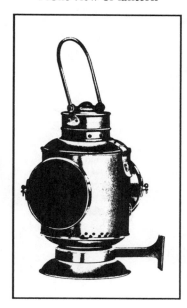

Nos. 46-51 Coach and Caboose Markers or Tail Lamps
Pre-1899 design.

Lower draft air flow system.

One, two, three, or four lenses. Lenses and glass in white, red, and green combinations, as shown.

Signal position A, B, C, D.

Viewed from above

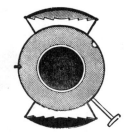

No. 46.
One smooth-face red lens, one smooth-face green lens.

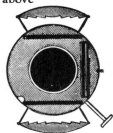

No. 47.
Two smooth-face white lenses, with two pieces each red and green glass.

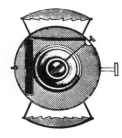

No. 48.
One smooth-face white lens, one smooth-face red lens, with two pieces green glass.

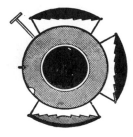

No. 49.
One smooth-face red lens, two smooth-face green lenses.

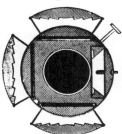

No. 50.
Three smooth-face white lenses, with three pieces each red and green glass.

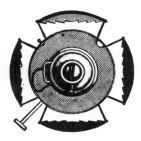

No. 51.
One smooth-face white lens, two smooth-face green lenses, one smooth-face red lens, or one smooth-face red lens, and three smooth-face green lenses.

Front view of lantern

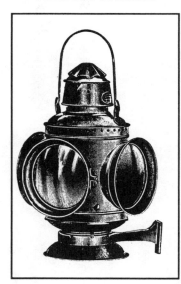

Nos. 53-58 Coach and Caboose Markers or Tail Lamps

Post 1904 design.

One, two, three, or four lenses and white, red, and green lenses or glass as shown.

This top-of-the-line lantern had a highly touted air-flow system called a Watt's Draft Ventilation, and was marked "WV" on its top. This ventilation system minimized the condensation or, in cold weather, the ice buildup inside the lantern, which blocked light and caused rust.

Signal position A, B, C, D.

Viewed from above

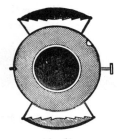

No. 53.
One smooth-face red lens, one smooth-face green lens.

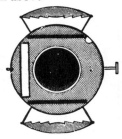

No. 54.
Two smooth-face white lenses, with two pieces each red and green glass.

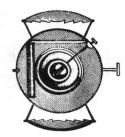

No. 55.
One smooth-face white lens, one smooth-face red lens, with two pieces green glass.

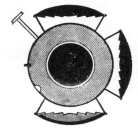

No. 56.
One smooth-face red lens, two smooth-face green lenses.

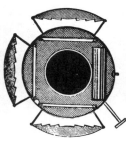

No. 57.
Three smooth-face white lenses, with three pieces each red and green glass.

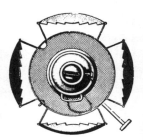

No. 58.
One smooth-face white lens, two smooth-face green lenses, one smooth-face red lens, or one smooth-face red lens, and three smooth-face green lenses.

No. 60 Tail Lamp
Post-1899 design.

5 3/8" ruby lens.

No. 193 Square Body Tail Lamp
(Not shown.)
Post-1899 design.

Similar to the No. 60 but with a different rear hanger.

Signal position B or D.

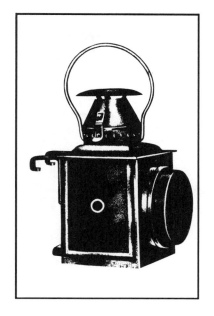

No. 191 Round Body,
Steel Cupola Lamp
Post-1899 design.

Two 5" white lenses.

Installed through the roof of the caboose, the signal colors could be changed from inside the car.

Signal position E.

No. 29 Combination Caboose Tail Lamp
Post-1899 design.

Figure A

"This lamp is placed in position from inside the caboose, and hence is easily trimmed, filled, and light adjusted from within while train is in motion. Its supply of air is received from interior of car, while the products of combustion escape through an outlet at top of lamp. There is no inlet from outside the car, therefore the light is unaffected when lamp is under heavy air pressure. Figure A shows the two inside compartments. When train is on main track, the light is placed in lower compartment, and displays a red signal to the rear and green ahead and at the side. When train is side-tracked, by transferring light to upper compartment, a green signal is shown in each of three directions side, front and rear."

No. 190 Round Body, Steel Revolving Caboose Cupola Lamp
Post-1899 design.

One 6" ruby lens, one 6" green lens. A steel slide "blinded" the red lens when only green was desired.

Signal position E.

No. 27 Caboose Cupola Lamp
Pre-1899 design.

Showed red from both ends. A tin cap was placed over the end pointing toward the engine, varying according to the direction in which the train was going.

Signal position E.

All three of these lamps (Nos. 191, 190, 27) were installed on its roof and operated from inside the caboose.

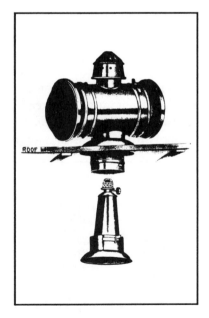

No. 26 Caboose Cupola Lamp
Pre-1899 design.

This had three compartments into which the oil pot could be placed, according to which signal was desired. When the train was on the main track, the oil pot was placed in the compartment showing green ahead and ruby to the rear. When the train was side-tracked, the oil pot was placed in the center compartment and displayed green both forward and rear. The middle compartment showed nothing.

Electrified Railroad Signal Lamps

Safety regulations for steam trains, which used lanterns for light, required that engine headlights and various warning signals be reliable, that is, that they burn consistently over a relatively long period, and not blow out easily. Some lanterns were found not to meet these standards very well and were removed from use, as unreliable for railroads. However, once trains were electrified, power for light came from the train generators. Adlake then re-introduced the lamps (No. 19 to No. 130) on the following pages, without the font and, instead, electrified. They were cheaper to make this way and continued in use for some years. Thus, you may come across these lamps, which appear to date from the 1870s to the 1890s, with an electric

bulb socket. This means that it is a twentieth century lantern although its design is Pre-1899. If you find one of these lamps with an oil font, it is a nineteenth century lantern.

No. 19 Square Body Tin Tail Lamp
Pre-1899 design.

4" ruby lens.

Signal position: rear of train.

No. 39 Square Body Signal Lamp

Pre-1899 design.

One or two 4" lens.

By 1907, offered with electric-light fixture only.

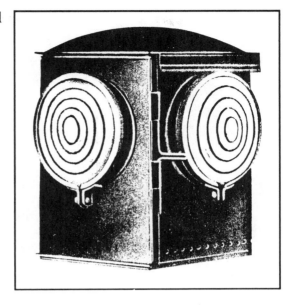

No. 94 Round Body
Tin Corner Stationary Marker

Pre-1899 design.

One 3" lens of any color desired.

Sold as a route designator.

No. 20 Square Body Tin Tail Lamp
Pre-1899 design.

*Two lenses (probably colored),
set at right angles.*

No. 21 (Not shown.)

*Similar to No. 20 but lenses set
opposite each other.*

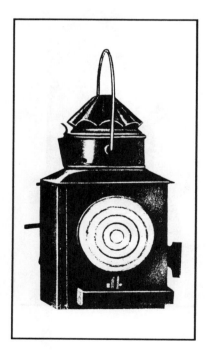

No. 22 Square Body Tin Tail Lamp
Pre-1899 design.

4" ruby lens.

No. 24 Tin Tail Lamp
Pre-1899 design.

Two 3" or 4" lenses set at right angles.

No. 23 (not shown), is similar, but with lenses set opposite each other.

Lenses available in several colors.

No. 214 Tin Tail Lamp
Pre-1899 design.

4" ruby lens.

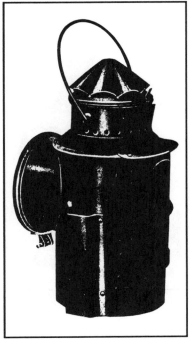

No. 183 Tail Lamp
Post-1899 design.

One 5" or 5 3/8" white lens.
Colored-glass panes slid between clear lens
and flame, giving color desired.

Equipped for red, green, or white signal.

No. 168 Steel Marker or Tail Lamp
Post-1899 design.

One, two, three, or four lenses of colors
(red, green, white) and size desired.
Lens sizes 4" to 7".

No. 161, 208 and 209 Round Body, Steel Tail Lamp
Post-1899 design.

4" or 5 3/8" lenses, other sizes available.

Sliding door gave access to lens for changing colors.

Nos. 161, 208 (not shown), and **209** (not shown) were similar lanterns, distinguished by their styles of mounting bracket.

No. 130 Tail Lamp
Post-1899 design.

5 3/8" white lens, heavy steel construction.

Hinged side door permitted insertion of colored glass behind lens to change colors.

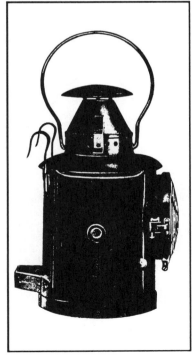

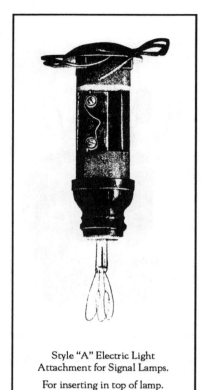

Style "A" Electric Light
Attachment for Signal Lamps.

For inserting in top of lamp.

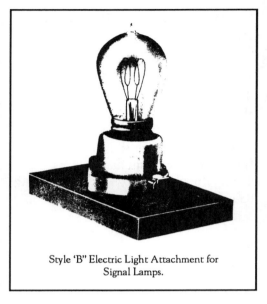

Style 'B' Electric Light Attachment for
Signal Lamps.

These electrified fixtures were offered as
replacements for oil fonts. They could fit
into the font position within the lamp.

Bridge Lamps

The lanterns (No. 101 to No. 199) on
the next few pages were for lighting
railroad bridges.

No. 101 Round Body
Steel Bridge Lamp
Post-1899 design.

*Two 6 3/8" ruby and two
6 3/8" green lenses.
Also available with 8" lenses.*

No. 200 Lift-Bridge Lamp

Post-1899 design.

8", 180-degree, white Fresnel lens.

Heavy steel construction.

Red and green glasses stored in the framework.

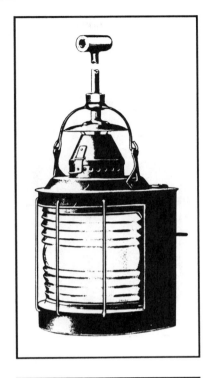

No. 196 Channel Sheerboom or Coast Lamp

Pre-1899 design.

8", 360-degree, white, green, or ruby Fresnel lens.

This could be seen from every direction.

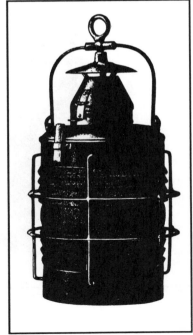

No. 197 Pier or Abutment Lamp
Post-1899 design.

Similar to the No. 200 lantern, but with a ruby Fresnel lens.

No. 199 Drawbridge Lamp
Post-1899 design.

Four 8" clear Fresnel lenses or two 8 3/8" red and two 8 3/8" green flat lenses.

Heavy steel construction.

Telegraph Train Order Signals

Called a "telegraph train order signal" because it was operated by the telegraph operator who was in contact with the next station, each of the three systems had a different mechanism for operating the signal lamp. Each had the same purpose, however. In the event of a problem on the line, or other messages, the operator could use the signal to halt the train in the station and pass information to the engineer, who would otherwise go straight through.

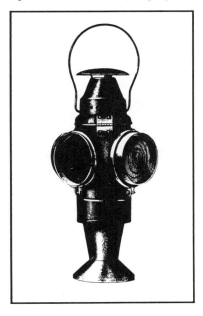

No. 61 Pressed Steel Lamp

For use on Nunn, Swift, or Cowdery train order signal.

This large lamp was located on top of the signal arm.

Nunn's Telegraph Train Order Signal

"The normal position of this signal is 'danger', making it reliable and effective. Day signal-blade and lamp are mounted at end of arm extending from station to any desired distance. Signals set from operator's desk. It has no springs or delicate machinery liable to get out of order. A brass cap covering the roller protects the working parts from the weather.

By change in construction this signal can be adapted for a double-track signal, which will hold train from one direction while giving the right-of-way from another direction; or trains from both directions can be held or given the right-of-way at same time."

Lamp Location

Lamp
Location

Swift's Telegraph Train Order Signal

"It is worked from the operator's desk, and he knows whether the signal is at 'danger' or 'clear'. When there are no orders for trains, the target is parallel with the track and cannot be seen. The target is shown at right angles with the track (as illustrated in cut) when trains are to be held 'for orders'. At night, a white or green light is shown with the 'no orders' or parallel position of target, and a red light is shown when trains are 'to be held'. It is changed in the same way as the target or day signal."

Cowdery's Telegraph Train Order Signal

"An effective signal, manipulated by the telegraph operator from his desk. Its use on the railroads which have adopted it has demonstrated its utility. It is always reliable, requiring neither weights, pulleys, strings, chains, wire, nor rope in its operation. There are no intricate parts to get out of order, and it shows at all times a positive signal of either 'danger' or 'clear'.

Lamp
Location

The signal always remains plumb and works perfectly.

It is not affected by the warping of the wooden arm.

A metallic covering protects the gearing from sleet and snow.

The signal works freely, showing either at right angles to or parallel with the track, a positive danger or safety signal."

Semaphore and Train Order Signal Lanterns

The lanterns (No. 7 to No. 6) on the next few pages, were heavily constructed to withstand hard use. They were used not by the telegrapher, but by personnel in the railroad yard and on the edge of the track, to signal warnings of problems (work in progress, track repairs, etc.).

No. 7 Square Body Semaphore Lamp
Pre-1899 design.

*One 5 3/8" white lens and one
2" bull's-eye lens.*

Side-door access to font.

No. 107 Harrington Semaphore Lamp
Pre-1880 design.

An early semaphore lamp.

Distant Signal Lamps
Pre-1899.

These two large lamps could be seen from a long way off.

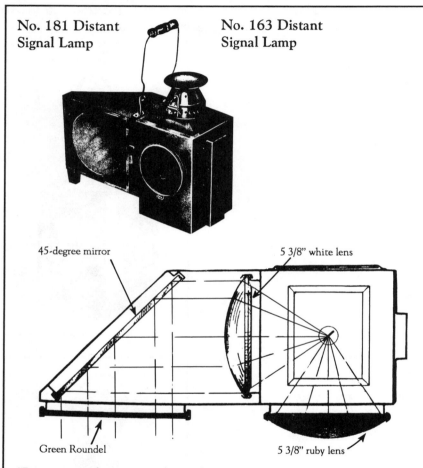

No. 181 Distant Signal Lamp

No. 163 Distant Signal Lamp

45-degree mirror

5 3/8" white lens

Green Roundel

5 3/8" ruby lens

"Projects two distinct signaling colors in parallel, using only one burner.

One-day or long-time burner. Prism glass reflectors with long-time burner, if desired.

Equipped with one 5 3/8" ruby lens; one 6 3/8" green roundel; one 5 3/8" white lens; one plate-glass mirror.

Face has one 5 3/8" ruby lens and one 6 3/8" green roundel displaying parallel combined red and green signals, signifying caution, when Semaphore arm is in corresponding position. When arm moves to clear position, steel blank in Semaphore casting blinds red lens, permitting only green or clear signal to be displayed."

No. 220 Combination Oil and Electric Semaphore Lamp
1906 – 1940.

Came with or without rear lens and could be fitted with lens of any size. A prism glass reflector was also an option.

Heavy steel construction.

When used as an electric lamp, it was connected to the train for power; it did not operate on batteries. Because of its dual funtion, it could be used on both steam and electrified trains.

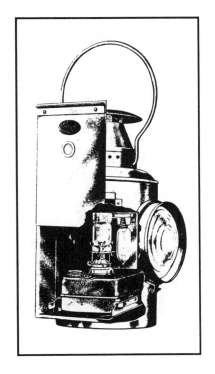

No. 9 Round-Body Steel Semaphore Lamp
Post 1899 design.

Came with or without rear lens; could be fitted with lens of any size.

Sliding-door access to burner.

No. 10 lamp was similar to the No. 9, but with two lenses back to back; came with a metallic or prism glass reflector. (Not shown.)

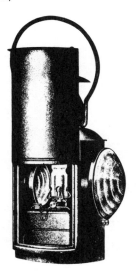

Font inside the No. 9 lamp.

No. 207 Round-Body Train Order Signal Lamp
Post-1899 design.

Two lenses, from 3" to 7", interchangeable with other colored lenses and disks.

Disk rim painted same color as lens (e.g., red or green) for daylight signaling. Glass or metal reflectors an option.

No. 204 Pressed-Steel Semaphore Lamp
Post-1899 design.

Hinged top for ease in cleaning burner.

Bracket mounting on side.

No. 81 Bottom-Draft Round-Body Semaphore Lamp
Pre-1899 design.

One 5 3/8" white lens and one 2" bull's-eye lens.

Tin or steel.

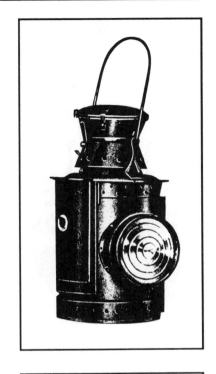

No. 3 Pressed-Steel Semaphore Lamp
Post-1899 design.

Two 4 1/8" lenses set opposite each other.

Oil font inserted from bottom; unusual.

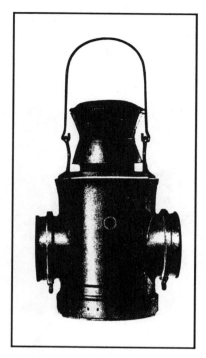

No. 82 Round-Body Train Order Lamp
Pre-1899 design.

Two 5 3/8" lenses.

Tin or steel.

No. 6 Square-Body Semaphore Lamp
Pre-1899 design.

*One 5 3/8" white lens and one
2" bull's-eye lens.*

Side-panel access to font.

Switch Lamps

Switch Lamps, (No. 73 to No. 169 1/2 on the next few pages) were located at line junctions called "points" and indicated to the engineer which way the points were directed so that he knew which track the train would go onto. These lanterns were offered with one-day or long-time burners.

No. 73 Switch Lamp
Pre-1899 design.

Three 5" lenses.

Sliding-door panel access to font. (Not shown.)

Made of steel.

No. 63 Pressed-Steel Switch Lamp
Post-1899 design.

Two lenses 4 1/2" and 4 1/8", or 4 1/2" with 5 3/8" lens.

Font inserted from bottom.

Unusually strong body, made from two pressed, heavy steel plates clamped and bolted together.

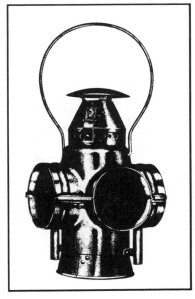

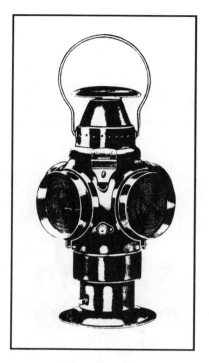

No. 169 Pressed Steel Lamp
Post-1899 design.

Two or four lenses.
4", 4 1/8", 4 1/2", 5", or 5 3/8" lens.
Outside wick adjuster.

Hinged top for cleaning. No. 169 also made as stronger model with supports between base and body. (Shown.)

No. 169 with base supports.

No. 169 1/2 Pressed-Steel Lamp
Post-1899 design.

Similar to the No. 169 but had red and white painted disks, for day signals.

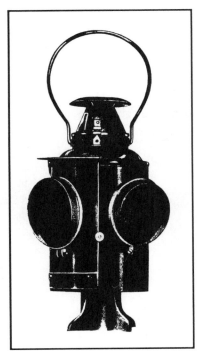

No. 206 Round Body Steel Switch Lamp
Post-1899 design.

Two 5" and two 4 1/2" lenses. Outside wick adjuster.

Sliding-panel access to font. (Not shown.)

Cab Lamps

No. 10 Cab Lamp
Ca. 1900.

Finish: Tin.

No. 5 Cab Lamp
Ca. 1900.

Finish: Brass or tin.

More commonly called gauge lamps by other companies.

Used in the engine cab by the fireman or engineer.

Miscellaneous Lamps

The lanterns illustrated in the remainder of this Adlake section were offered as a complement to the general sales line, for use by guards, or on platforms.

Tubular Station Lamp
1880 – 1914.

Came in three sizes:

No. (1): No. 1 burner, 5/8" wick, 6" silvered-glass reflector.

No. (2): No. 2 burner, 1" wick, 7" silvered-glass reflector.

No. (3): No. 3 burner, 1 1/2" wick, 12" silvered-glass reflector.

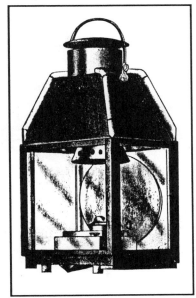

No. 3 Globe Platform Lamp
Manufactured prior to 1899; until well into the 1920s.

Height: 25".
No 3. burner, 1 1/2" wick.
Finish: painted black.

A hanging version with a bail also was available.

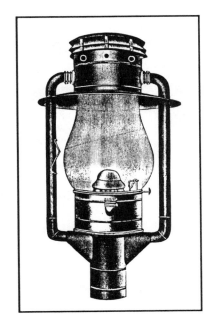

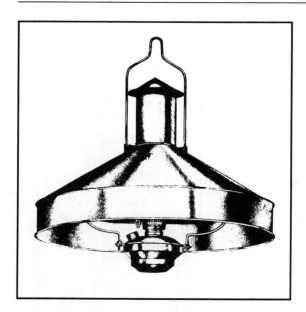

No. 166 Center Tower Lamp

Diameter of reflector: 22 1/2".
No. 2 solar burner.

An overhead light for stations.

No. 53 1/2 Bracket Lamp
1870 – 1920s.

Glass or tin font; heavy bronze font also available. Came with a silvered-glass reflector.

For station waiting rooms.

No 163 Desk Lamp
1870 to 1920's

No. 2 burner.

*Polished brass bowl and japanned
iron stand.*

No. 1 Station Platform Lamp
1880 – 1913.

*Adlake made three different models of the
No. 1 Station Platform Lamp.*

*No. l: square body, 9" by 12" windows,
8" reflector.*

*No. 2: square body, 10" by 14" windows,
8" reflector.*

*No. 3: triangular body (not shown),
10" by 14" windows, 8" reflector.*

Finish: heavy tin.

Made expressly for the railway service.

Policeman's or Watchman's Dark Lamp
Early 1900s.

Finish: brass or heavy tin.

Tri-Color Lamp
1880 – 1930.

"For track walkers, taking the place of three lanterns. It has a revolving cylinder inside carrying red and green signals; operated from without by the bail, and fixed in position by means of a flat spring at the back, with stop catch."

The bail mechanism changed the lamp colors. Unusual.

Lovell-Dressel

Little information is available on this company's products. It made mostly railroad lanterns and apparently merged with Lovell at some point. Very rare, they are marked "Dressel" on top.

No. 30

DECK CABOOSE LAMP.

PATENTED.

THIS LAMP CAN BE REVOLVED TO ANY DESIRED POSITION FROM THE INTERIOR OF THE CABOOSE.

THE POSITION OF THE SIGNALS ARE DETERMINED BY THE LOWER CYLINDER, WHICH IS PAINTED TO CORRESPOND WITH THE LENS COLORS.

NO WATER CAN ENTER THE CAR, THE RESTING PLATES BEING STAMPED WITH FLANGES, AND ARE MADE OF HEAVY GALVANIZED STEEL.

IS FURNISHED WITH TWO OR FOUR LENSES 8 INCHES DIAM., OR ANY OTHER SIZE AS MAY BE DESIRED.

THE LAMP CAN BE LIGHTED AND CLEANSED FROM THE INTERIOR OF THE CABOOSE.

BROKEN OR ANY DESIRED COLOR LENSES CAN BE REPLACED BY THE USE OF OUR IMPROVED LENS HOLDERS, AS APPLIED TO ALL OF OUR LAMPS.

NOW STANDARD ON SEVERAL OF THE LARGEST RAILROADS.

Samples and Prices Furnished on Application.

A rare catalog illustration from Dressel sales material.
No. 30 Deck Caboose Lamp, Ca. 1900.

Section III:

Managing Your Lantern Collection

Locating, Identifying, and Pricing Lanterns

Where might you find lanterns? Obvious places are flea markets, tag sales, antique stores, railroad memorabilia shows, and museums. Obviously, the latter will not sell you lanterns, but they do give you the opportunity to see and study lantern models that you might never see elsewhere. This will help you gain experience at spotting and evaluating the rarer lanterns.

You may come across lanterns in many other contexts. They are still used for decoration or, often electrified, as post and porch lights. They decorate beams in restaurants and hide in corners of barns and basements. Some people keep a few around their house in case of a power failure. And, as other people learn that you are interested in lanterns, they will make a point of telling you where they have seen them.

Identifying

Some of the lanterns you encounter randomly might be worth buying. If you familiarize yourself with the illustrations in this book, you will develop a sense of which lanterns are common and which are rare.

Be aware, for instance, of what a streamlined lantern style looks like. These lanterns can resemble 19th-century models, but their crimp marks, from the newer manufacturing process, betray their 20th-century origins.

Look for the maker's name or the model name or number somewhere on the bell or font, or even on the globe or underneath the base. Use one or more of these, and the illustrations in this book, to narrow down the lantern type, or even the actual lantern model and approximate date.

Be especially careful when trying to date a lantern by a patent date stamped on it. Remember that the lantern might have been made over a twenty-year period with the same patent date stamp. Note also that some manufacturer's patent date stamps can refer to only a small part on the lantern (e.g., size of globe plate hole, and bail shape). (See pp. 29-30.) Thus, a lantern may have been manufactured ten years after the patent date stamped on it, but, for the sake of prestige, the manufacturer kept stamping older patent dates to show, as a kind of advertisement, how many patents applied to it.

Also confusing is the discovery of a patent date on a lantern that is later than the last production date given in the specifications section. This may indicate that the manufacturer had a large order for a special run of a lantern that was out of production and added a later patent date, applicable to some minor improvement, when the special order was run. Or, it may mean that the manufacturer had a stock of no-longer-produced lanterns that were dug out of mothballs and reworked, with a minor improvement warranting a new patent date, and put back on the market as a reintroduction.

If the lantern is not illustrated in this book but there is a manufacturer's name and address stamped on it, write to the Town Clerk or City Directory there. They probably can tell you the dates the manufacturer was in business.

If you find a lantern you cannot date because there is no manufacturers or patent date stamp on it (e.g., Rayo No. 3), look up its similar type in the Dietz section and add three years. This gives you a reasonably accurate date of production start, because Dietz led the field in design and style, and was copied by most other companies. (That is, Dietz probably made it first.)

Materials and Finishes

Next, try to establish the material and finish. The specifications usually list possible finishes. Refer to the section "Materials, Finishes, and Markings" for help in making subtle distinctions.

The difficult question, if it is painted, is whether the color is original. A study of shipping records shows that, apart from rare special orders, the color shipped by most manufacturers was black. There were exceptions. A notable one was the Embury Lantern Company, which preferred dark green. However, many customers, especially large users, painted their lanterns a color different from the original one, for identification purposes.

Another question is whether this paint, or the original paint, is covering a nice copper font or a brass top, which could make the lantern more valuable. Always carry a small magnet with you to test painted lanterns when you are "shopping." Some metals will react to the magnet, and some will not. You can determine whether there is copper, brass, or steel under the paint because the magnet will not adhere to copper or brass as it does to steel, tin or other metals with high ferrous content. Nickel-plated brass and copper can also be detected this way.

In general, be cautious and do your homework. You may need to measure, check markings and styles, evaluate finishes and materials, compare it to similar lanterns, and check minor distinguishing features noted in this book, in order to pin down a lantern's identity.

Condition

Besides identifying the lantern, you will need to assess its condition. You might want it no matter what shape it is in, if it is rare or a model you have specifically been looking for. But the worse the condition, the more it affects the price. Check out the metal for dents, cracks, and rust, especially around the base of the font. Be thorough. Avoid buying a lantern that is so rusted through that you cannot paint or restore it. Check whether the glass globe has any cracks, and whether it fits correctly into the lantern's globe plate. (If it does not, it may be the wrong size.) Check the illustration to make sure it has the right shape. Many globes are substitutions from other lanterns. Does the illustration indicate a hood, or reflector, or mounting clamp that is not there now? This is a common omission, especially for glass reflectors. Are there any obviously broken parts? A side tube, a ratchet, etc.? Are they fixable?

Some lanterns have been electrified. As long as no hole has been drilled into the lantern — for example, to gain access for a wire through the font, or to add an off/on switch — the value has not been substantially reduced. If one has been drilled, unless it is a very rare lantern, do not buy it. Remember, also, that any lantern that has been electrified is now lacking its burner assembly, so it is missing an original, integral part.

Pricing

People ask me two things about lantern prices: what did the lantern cost when it was manufactured, and what should they pay for it today. To answer the first question, let us use as an example the Dietz No. 2 Tubular Lantern, which is probably the most common lantern you will come across.

In 1876, it retailed to the general public for $2.47. In 1881, it cost 78 cents; in 1888, 66 cents; in 1905, $1.60. Between the world wars, and up to 1950, it went for as high as $5.84, a tremendous variation, over the years. Other lanterns, such as the Dietz No. 17 Side Lamp, sold for $2.15 in 1876, while street lamps cost $4.04 each in the same year. Lanterns sold to railroads seem to have been higher priced: for example, the No. 39 and Vesta series sold from $2.00 to $3.00 each in 1913. Fire company lanterns were by far the most expensive. The King Fire brass lantern cost $7.08 in 1913 and $11.70 in 1940.

Over the last few years, lanterns have shown steady increases in price, reflecting the growing interest in the collecting of lanterns. Collectors are, of course, looking for rarer and rarer lanterns, which drives prices higher and higher. This will continue to be true.

To get some estimate of the price range for any particular lantern you are interested in, use the figures listed below. Contemporary prices asked by dealers are divided into four broad ranges. These categories are tied to the four ratings of comparative rarity given to the lanterns mentioned in this book. The prices are not "firm," since they vary according to location, condition, and market demand. But they will give you an idea of what to expect, in the next few years, when shopping for lanterns. It is assumed that the lanterns are in fairly good condition for these prices.

Very Common	$10.00 to $ 45.00
Common	$25.00 to $ 70.00
Rare	$70.00 to $200.00
Very Rare	$200.00 to $500.00

Besides the specific ratings of comparative rarity given in the individual lantern specifications, you will do well to keep in mind some general conditions that make most lanterns rarer.

- Brass or copper; the latter being rarer.
- Silver or gold; silver-plated or gold-plated.
- Lanterns made prior to 1890.
- Globe color: blue, green, and amber are rarest; clear and red, common.
- Globe professionally etched with the owner's name.
- Intact color disk inside fire lanterns.
- Glass font lantern in pristine condition.

Lantern Repair and Restoration

Whether you wish to clean your lantern up a bit and whether you do any repair or restoration, and the degree to which you do it, will depend upon the condition of the lantern, whether you want a "working" lantern, and how "new" you want it to look.

To begin restoration, first remove the globe and the burner and wick assembly of your new lantern. Take out the old wick and discard it. Wash all the parts, including the globe and burner, in hot, soapy, water. This will remove the years' accumulation of soot and oily dirt. Washing will not harm the lantern, while substantially improving its appearance.

Repairing and Cleaning

If the lantern has broken parts, this is the time to repair them. With hand-soldered (not "streamlined") lanterns, you can hand-solder the parts back together or get someone to do it for you. Use the parts-and-specification sections of this book to guide you. You need to do this soldering with some finesse (the parts can be very small and the metal thin), but it can be done and will restore the lantern to working condition.

As a possible replacement for solder, you can use one of the excellent epoxy glues now available. However, if you intend to make this a working lantern, use solder, not epoxy glues. Dents in metal parts can be filled in with epoxy filler if you wish to remove them. Smooth the surface afterward, sanding with fine sandpaper. (Dents usually affect a lantern's appearance but not its function.)

To remove rust from a lantern, use fine emery paper and steel wool. Even Brillo or SOS pads are helpful. Unlacquered brass or copper lanterns often have a patina, from age, that is hard to remove. Standard cleaners do not usually take it away. If the lantern is a valuable one, you should have it professionally cleaned. Otherwise, use soft cloths to clean and buff the lantern so that you do not scratch it.

Restoring Finishes

To completely restore a painted lantern, you must first decide whether the paint is original. Remember that the paint you see could be the original paint put on by the manufacturer, a second coat put on by the user, or a second or third coat put on by someone who tried to restore the lantern. Remove a small chip of paint to establish the original color. Then decide if you wish to strip off all the paint and repaint it the original color for authenticity.

You may also wish to remove paint if you have found a lantern made wholly or in part of brass or copper. Such lanterns were usually lacquered or polished by the factory, rather than painted, so you can assume that this is not original paint. Shiny and dull spots on a lantern are an indication of peeling lacquer, which cannot be polished. You can use most of the usual paint strippers on painted or lacquered lanterns, but follow the manufacturers' directions carefully. You will need a small brush to get the paint stripper into all the nooks and crannies of a lantern. Follow up by washing in hot water. To paint the lantern use a spray paint, which will get into all the crevices where parts meet. Or, if it is brass or copper, you may apply clear lacquer.

Nickel-plated brass or copper is the other finish you will commonly find in lanterns. Nickel is very shiny and pretty when first applied. Because of age and wear, this finish usually is in poor condition. It looks dull and has no shine, so it resembles the regular tin finish. Except by having it nickel-plated again by a plating company, you cannot restore this kind of finish. An alternative is to take the lantern to a metal-polishing company, where the nickel plate can be stripped off to expose the metal underneath. This should be done only by a professional, because dangerous acids are used in the process.

Replacement Parts

You can usually use the existing burner on an old lantern, but if you cannot, replacement burners and wicks are available in most hardware stores. Use the specifications given in this book to match or approximate the original size and type. Fitzall globes can be bought from many hardware stores and at flea markets. Also, electric fittings are available in hardware stores if you wish to use your lantern as an electric lamp. Remember, if you do this, not to drill holes into it or change it in any way. You will reduce its value if you do.

Having cautioned you to buy only lanterns that are in very good condition, I must note that there are always exceptions. At a flea market, I once saw, and bought, a very rare Dietz No. 00 Tubular Lantern (1870 to 1874) that had no globe, a broken side tube, and a dented oil font. I stripped off all the paint, down to the bare metal, repaired, by soldering, all the broken parts, filled and sanded the dents, and then spray painted it with a black semigloss. Crowned with a Fitzall globe, it is now a fine addition to my collection.

Routine Lantern Care

About 1900, Adams and Westlake published these instructions for lantern care. If you have a working lantern collection, they will be as helpful today as they were at the turn of the century.

1. Oil — All our lamps are equipped for burning kerosene oil, unless otherwise specified.

2. Cleaning — The lamp should be thoroughly cleaned, inside and out; the lenses should be left perfectly clean, and all soot and dirt should be removed from inside of lamp, and from the ventilator openings.

3. Trimming Wick — The wick should not be trimmed with shears, but the charred portion should be broken off with the fingers or with a stick, the wick being turned down so that only the charred portion is exposed above the wick tube. Should the wick fray out at the edges during this operation, it can be slightly trimmed off with shears.

4. Filling — In filling the fount, a space of from 1/8 to 1/4 of an inch at the top of the fount should be left unfilled. This will give room for expansion of the oil as it becomes heated after the lamp is lighted, and will prevent the flooding of the flame with the oil, which would otherwise be forced up through the wick tube if the fount were filled full, and would either cause the lamp to burn with a high and smoky flame, or possibly cause an explosion and the burning out of the lamp.

5. Lighting — When the lamp is first lighted, the flame should be turned up to about one-half the height required to give the full light, and be thus allowed to burn for ten or fifteen minutes so that all parts can become thoroughly warmed, after which the flame can be adjusted to the height which gives the best light, and the lamp then placed in position.

If the flame is turned up to the height giving the best light before the wick tube and fount become warmed, as soon as they are warmed a large amount of oil will be carried through the wick and supplied to the flame, thereby causing it to burn too high and to smoke, filling the inside of the lamp with soot and rendering the light useless.

6. Oil Tanks and Receptacles should be thoroughly cleansed at stated periods, as sediment will collect and in time will be of sufficient quantity to deteriorate the oil. This results in lamps giving poor service.

7. New wicks — It is the office of the wick to convey the oil from the fount to the flame. It acts as a strainer and in time accumulates a considerable quantity of dirt and thick, gummy oil. This accumulation prevents that ready and smooth flow of oil which is necessary to the maintenance of a steady and uniform flame. As soon, therefore, as the wick becomes dirty and stiff from this accumulation, it should be thrown away and a new one put in its place. Long time burner wicks should be changed every two months, or oftener if dirty or stiff.

8. The Long-Time Burner — Lamps fitted with long-time burners should be attended to regularly. This is usually done two or three times per week, at stated intervals.

9. Chimneys for Long-Time Burners — The Chimney should be cleaned with waste or paper ONLY and should not be washed. If it becomes broken, it should be replaced immediately.

Glossary

Bail A wire handle.

Bell A lantern top.

Bow The front section of a boat.

Brass An alloy of zinc and copper.

Bronzed Coated with an alloy of copper and tin which gave a yellow to olive-brown color.

Bull's Eye A thick circular piece of glass.

Buoy A float moored on water as a channel or danger marker.

Candlepower Luminous intensity, a measure of brightness.

Canopy A lantern top.

Char The burned area of a wick.

Copper A reddish-brown metal.

Corrugated Glass or metal molded into alternating ridges and grooves.

Crimped Metal pressed into small folds or ridges to provide stiffness and strength.

Dash The panels on the side and front of a carriage or automobile.

Dome A lantern top.

Font The oil reservoir.

Fresnel A lens made in such a way as to amplify and focus light more strongly.

Girandole A fancy candle holder.

Globe A glass protective covering over the flame.

Government Globe A lantern made to government – usually Federal – specifications.

Guard A wire encircling the globe to protect the globe from breakage.

Hindi A language spoken in northern India.

Japan A type of enamel or lacquer paint finish originating in the orient.

Lens A molded glass.

Mild Steel A soft, malleable metal.

Nickel-Plate An even layer of nickel deposited on metal surfaces by dipping or electroless plating.

Patent Date The date of a grant issued by the government to an inventor assuring him the sole right to make, use, and sell his invention.

Re-dipped After lantern was assembled the completed lantern was dipped in a molten tin-lead mixture to recoat all surfaces as an added protection against corrosion.

Rigid Fiber Bail Bail was locked in the up position. Fiber was insulation for use in electric rail areas.

Sangster A type of locking clip attached to fonts; used on a variety of dead-flame lanterns.

Semaphore A visual signaling light or flag.

Spun Metal A mechanical process that gave a smooth shine to the metal.

Streamline The style name given to many Dietz lanterns manufactured after 1939 by a process of molding and crimping rather than hand soldering the parts together.

Bibliography

Baltimore and Ohio Magazine, February 1923. Issued to the employees of the Baltimore and Ohio Railroad.

Courter, J. W. *Aladdin Electric Lamps.* Simpson, Ill.: Privately published, 1987. Mr. Courter is a professor at the University of Illinois.

Dietz, G. Ulysses. *Dietz & Company 1840 Illustrated Catalog.* Watkins Glen, N.Y.: American Life Foundation, 1982. 124 pages. Mr. Dietz, a descendant of R. E. Dietz, is curator of the arts department of the Newark Museum, Newark, N.J.

R. E. Dietz Company. Syracuse, N.Y., 1913. *A Leaf From the Past.* (A collection of interesting passages from the Dietz diary.)

Drepperd, Carl, W. *A Dictionary of American Antiques.* Garden City, N.Y.: Doubleday, 1952. P. 225 illustration of lighting devices and lamps.

Gross, Leo, ed. *Key. Lock & Lantern.* A quarterly magazine published for many years and to date from Box 15, Spencerport, N.Y., for railroadiana collectors.

Gross, Joseph, and Richard Barrett. *The Railroad Lantern.* Forthcoming, 1991. Gives an extensive listing of American lantern manufacturers.

Hornung, Clarence P. *Treasury of American Design.* New York: Abrams, 1972. Pp. 315 – 33.

Sherwood, George and Ruth. *The Winchester Center Kerosene Lamp Museum.* Winchester Center, Conn. Eight-page booklet available from the museum.

Three Centuries of American Antiques. New York: Bonanza Books, 1979. Pp. 296 – 306.

Thuro, Catherine, M. *Oil Lamps.* Vols. 1 – 3. Toronto: Thorncliff House, 1983. 160 pages.

Watkins, C. Malcolm. "Lighting Devices." In *Concise Encyclopedia of American Antiques.* Edited by Helen Comstock. New York: Hawthorn Books. Pp. 215 – 23.

Index

Index of Individual Lanterns Listed By Manufacturers

The index lists individual lanterns which are mentioned and in most cases illustrated in the text. A list of manufacturers, with dates of operation where known, is given on pages 41-42.